THE MORTICIAN'S CHILD
The casket in our living room
the hearse outside the Dairy Queen
and the rest of my life six feet above

Kathleen L. Hawkins

Windsor Westcott
Publishing

The Mortician's Child

Copyright © by Kathleen L. Hawkins
www.WinningSpirit.com

Some of the names in this book have been changed to protect people's privacy.

Author's notes

The events in some of the chapters aren't necessarily in chronological order. I might start out as a child in one chapter, and then, in the same chapter, become a teenager or an adult thinking back on the events. In the next chapter, I might be a child again. In each case, I specify how old I was at the time—or at what point it was in my life—so readers can travel with me easily through time.

Disclaimer

The name Dairy Queen is trademarked. The name as it's used in this book is for identification purposes only; it's a place where the author and her father stopped for ice cream. Neither the publisher, author, nor this book are in any way affiliated with Dairy Queen. This book is not licensed, endorsed, or sponsored by Dairy Queen, nor does it necessarily represent their opinions or views.

All rights reserved. No part of this book may be reproduced in any form without written consent of the publisher.

ISBN: 978-0-9745452-3-3

1. Memoir 2. Psychology 3. Death 4. Mortician
5. Family 6. Kathleen L. Hawkins
I. Title

Also by Kathleen L. Hawkins

BOOKS

The Insiders (a novel)
We Know What You're Thinking
and the Truth will be Told

Speed Reading Made Easy
Read Faster, Remember More
Improve Your Comprehension

Spirit Incorporated
How to Follow Your Spiritual Path from 9 to 5
Whatever Your Job, Faith, or Challenge

Time Management Made Easy

Test Your Entrepreneurial IQ

AUDIO LEARNING PROGRAM

How to Organize Yourself to Win

Praise for The Mortician's Child

Winner of the Mayborn Nonfiction Prize
for Literary Excellence

The Mortician's Child surprises, horrifies, appeals to voyeuristic tendencies and, at the same time, tugs at our heartstrings. — Cindy Groom-Harry, CEO, CMC

Wow. Mesmerizing and fabulous. I enjoyed every minute of it. Kathleen has shared her life so beautifully. Humbly and lovingly, too. This is the kind of book the world needs, it is so real. — Cassandra Miosic, legal assistant

The Mortician's Child is wildly different from anything I've ever read. The writing is far more imaginative and goes way beyond a traditional memoir. I love it! — Dr. Lynne Kelly, author, *The Memory Code*

Fascinating. Kathleen is remarkably resilient and damn healthy given her situation. Any one of the events she experienced would screw up most people; she had one traumatic experience after another. And she doesn't drink or do drugs. It's a miracle.
— J. Johnson, teacher

Kathleen is incredible: far deeper, more intuitive, and more genuine than most people ever allow themselves to be. Thank you, Kathleen, for speaking about your soul, and in doing so, speaking to mine.
— R.G., Ph.D., Licensed Marriage and Family Therapist

Dedication

For Lissa

My first and forever friend

~~~

And for the young girl I was
who wrote in her diary every day.
You were a reporter, my memory.
I hope to be your wisdom.

Doesn't everything die at last, and too soon? Tell me, what is it you plan to do with your one wild and precious life? — Mary Oliver

There are years that ask questions and years that answer. — Zora Neale Hurston

THE MORTICIAN'S CHILD	1
KATHLEEN L. HAWKINS	1
WINDSOR WESTCOTT	1
PUBLISHING	1
THE MORTICIAN'S CHILD	2
COPYRIGHT © BY KATHLEEN L. HAWKINS	2
AUTHOR'S NOTES	2
DISCLAIMER	2
BOOKS	3
SPEED READING MADE EASY	3
SPIRIT INCORPORATED	3
TIME MANAGEMENT MADE EASY	3
TEST YOUR ENTREPRENEURIAL IQ	3
AUDIO LEARNING PROGRAM	3

HOW TO ORGANIZE YOURSELF TO WIN	3
PRAISE FOR THE MORTICIAN'S CHILD	4
WINNER OF THE MAYBORN NONFICTION PRIZE	4
THE MORTICIAN'S CHILD* IS WILDLY DIFFERENT FROM ANYTHING I'VE EVER READ. THE WRITING IS FAR MORE IMAGINATIVE AND GOES WAY BEYOND A TRADITIONAL MEMOIR. I LOVE IT! — DR. LYNNE KELLY, AUTHOR, *THE MEMORY CODE	4
FOR LISSA	5
AND FOR THE YOUNG GIRL I WAS	5
THERE ARE YEARS THAT ASK QUESTIONS AND	11
CONTENTS	11
YEARS THAT ASKED QUESTIONS	11
FUGUE . . . 3	12
SWITCHED AT BIRTH	12
INTO THE WILD DIVIDE	13
YEARS THAT ANSWERED	13
THE FOUNDATION	13
THE MYSTERY OF LOSS	13

EPILOGUE . . . 202	13
LINKS . . . 203	13
MOM AND DAD	1
THE MORTICIAN'S CHILD	1
OUR HOME IN BERKLEY, MICHIGAN, A DETROIT SUBURB	2
YEARS THAT ASKED QUESTIONS	3
FUGUE	3
— WEBMD.COM/MENTAL-HEALTH	3
SWITCHED AT BIRTH	7
1. INTO THE ABYSS	7
2. THE HOUR OF LEAD	14
4. MUCK FIRES AND FARM BOYS	26
6. MERRY CHRISTMAS	36
7. SNARL	44
I ASK MOM, "WHY'D DAD BECOME A MORTICIAN?"	46
8. THE SUMMONS	48
9. WHAT HE DOES IN THERE	49

10. THE WIGWAM	56
11. UNATTACHED CLUSTERS, IMPROPER SHUTDOWN	61
12. CUMBERLAND GAP	65
15. HAMMERHEAD STALL	81
16. THE PRESS BOX	90
20. THE FIRE UNDERNEATH	101
INTO THE WILD DIVIDE	104
21. YOU, YOU, YOU, AND YOU	104
22. HUNGER FOR THE VIVID	107
24. SÉANCE, LATE AFTERNOON	117
BEFORE THE SÉANCE	117
AFTER THE SÉANCE	119
25. *AHHH*, CHOCOLATE!	120
26. THE THING ITSELF	128
28. MAKING TRACKS	137
YEARS THAT ANSWERED	143
THE FOUNDATION	143

29. STANCHIONS	143
30. THE PHYSICIAN AND THE WITCH	144
THE MYSTERY OF LOSS	159
32. "WHAT A PARTY LINE!"	159
34. SCHUSTER	163
35. WOUNDED	165
REDEMPTION	168
36. THE JOURNALS	168
37. THE GIFT OF THE SPEED BUMP	176
38. HUSH LITTLE BABY, DON'T YOU CRY, I'LL SING YOU A LULLABY	178
39. CONNECTING THE DOTS	180
CONNECT-THE-DOTS PUZZLES, EASY, MEDIUM-HARD, AND DIFFICULT	180
40. EATING GOD	185
I WOULD RATHER LIVE MY LIFE AS IF THERE IS A GOD AND	185
41. ROCKSLIDE	187
42. LIKE MEDICINE	195

43. THE FINAL CONVERSATION	198
EPILOGUE	202
LINKS	203
RESTAURANTS	203
LAKES	203
BOB-LO ISLAND AMUSEMENT PARK AND STEAMSHIPS	203
UNIVERSITIES	203
WOMEN'S ARMY AUXILIARY CORPS (WAAC)	204
MUSIC	204
LGBTQ HISTORY AND REFERENCES	204
SPIRITUAL INFLUENCES	205
THOUGHTS, BLOGS, AND RESOURCES ABOUT DEATH	205
• CALEB WILDE, *CONFESSIONS OF A FUNERAL DIRECTOR* HTTPS://WWW.CALEBWILDE.COM	205
• PAMELA SKJOLSVIK, "THE DEATH WRITER," AUTHOR OF *DEATH BECOMES US* AND *FOREVER 51* HTTPS://WWW.PAMELASKJOLSVIK.COM/BOOKS	205

Mom and Dad
Ages 23 and 24

The mortician's child

Two funeral homes where I lived before I was six years old

Our home in Berkley, Michigan, a Detroit suburb

YEARS THAT ASKED QUESTIONS

Fugue

"Dissociative fugue" is one of a group of conditions called "dissociative disorders" ... People with fugue temporarily lose their sense of personal identity ... Outwardly [they] show no signs of illness, such as odd behavior ...

Dissociative fugue has been linked to severe stress, which might be the result of traumatic events that the person experienced or witnessed ... Most fugues are brief, lasting from less than a day to several months. Often, the disorder goes away on its own.
— Webmd.com/mental-health

Our sense of worth, of well-being, even our sanity depends upon our remembering. But, alas, our sense of worth, our well-being, our sanity also depends upon our forgetting.
— Joyce Appleby

Amnesia is like opening a suitcase and discovering that I picked up the wrong luggage at the baggage claim after a flight. I see a sweater, slacks, and toiletries, but nothing familiar. These items must belong to someone else.

I've sprung fully-grown—blinking and bewildered—into a strange, bright afternoon, steering a teal-blue Camaro through traffic. In the rearview mirror I see serious, blue-gray eyes with perfectly arched brows. I run fingers through long hair, pull it forward: dark strawberry blonde, almost auburn, straight, and silky. On the seat next to me, two books: *The Future of Time* and *The Haunted Mind*.

I'm wearing a beige skirt, a cream-colored silk blouse, and sturdy, brown high heels.

Rumbling past me are muddy 18-wheelers hauling shiny new cars, and on both sides of the freeway, there are gently sloping brown hills, and fields laced with side roads and dotted with maple trees and puddles where the land is low.

Amnesia isn't empty. It's shallow like rainwater in those puddles spiked with weeds, reflecting only the present: birds that sweep across an expansive blue sky, and a stranger who walks along the side of the road going for gas or help.

I want to exit and take a side road, but which one leads to my life? If there's no beginning here, is there no end? Am I suspended in the forever present, driving the pavement of a beautiful day?

Is someone waiting for me to return from a coffee break? Did a friend, lover, or a relative stop thinking about me for a second and I ceased to exist? Even my breathing is shallow. I inhale deliberately and deeply and then exhale slowly to try to steady myself. It's terrifying in this vacuum. I continue to drive, not a threat to anyone's safety. I know what traffic signs and signals mean and I obey.

The coffee shop has no name—like me—but a sign brags FINE FOOD. I exit onto Middlebelt Road. "Middlebelt, Middlebelt, Middlebelt," I repeat like a mantra or a password to commit the name to a new reserve of memories or conjure up the old.

Middlebelt must be the center of a town or city, a division between two sections—the median between memory and mystery? I'm driving the narrow line.

The cars in the FINE FOOD parking lot have Michigan license plates. I park, go in, and sit down. The server hands me a laminated menu that tells me I'm in "Dearborn Heights." A calendar on the wall says "April 1967," and a clock says "4:00." But calendars and clocks are meaningless. Progression of time is truly measured by feelings and collections; I have neither.

Customers sip coffee and read newspapers. Will any of them claim me as family, a friend, or maybe arrest me for a crime I don't remember committing?

"What?" I ask the server.

"Are you ready to order?" she repeats, apparently taken aback by my intensity.

"Coffee."

"Cream?" she asks suspiciously, as if sensing something's amiss.

"Yes."

I swirl it into the dark coffee and marvel at the rich compromise of colors. I pass up the sugar—a taste preference from my past? Does this body have memories it won't share with me?

The server looks up from polishing a pie case and smiles. I return her smile uneasily.

A poster on the wall tells restaurant personnel what to do if someone chokes, and under it, a mirror in which I confront myself: tall and slender with the same serious eyes I saw in the rearview mirror. Embarrassed to be an interloper in an unfamiliar body, a voyeur watching myself from a distance, I glance away.

I move cautiously as though memory is linked to a sense of balance and raise my cup for a refill. What an unpredictable place, a world in which one has no memories. Beware of ambush by people who know who they are, who have names, and who are certain of themselves.

I try to summon up a sense of the situation but realize with dread that intuition—as well as identity and balance—roots itself in memory. Oh God, give me an arsenal of memories—lurid or ecstatic, boring and insignificant, manic or depressive—and they'll give me an identity and a place in the world, give me whatever is truly mine and I'll be strong again.

I shiver. Am I safe here? Could I think my way out of a dangerous situation? Am I smart, or does intelligence also depend on memory? I can't let anyone know that I'm this lost. I'd be too vulnerable, a target. If I had a name, I'd have a chance.

"Cream of mushroom soup with whole wheat bread," I tell the server, and then think proudly, I made a decision, and the soup will be warm and friendly.

The sound of the bowl being set on the counter and the fragrant mushrooms and spices unlock something inside me, and to my great relief, memory returns, feeling not guilty for having strayed. It comes without direction or apology and fills me everywhere at once with its objects, a whole life with a history: baby books with bold colors, cider mills in the autumn, a bicycle, college, awards, writing scholarships, degrees, and, yes, a family, profession, and lovers. I'm 21 years old. I have an identity and a life—dark with secrets and silences, full of passion—with skeletons in its closet.

I wanted to get away from it, but I've been thrown back into the briar patch. And now, only after remembering, I realize there were a few things that I needed to forget.

SWITCHED AT BIRTH

1. Into the Abyss
When you gaze long into the Abyss, the Abyss
also gazes into you. — Friedrich Nietzsche

Stephen King and I were switched at birth. How do I know? Because I saw an interview with him on TV and the interviewer asked what kind of childhood he had, and he shrugged and said it was fairly normal. It was then I knew that Steven King got the childhood I should have had, and I got the childhood of a horror writer. I was the daughter of a freelance mortician who worked for 22 funeral homes throughout the Detroit area and suburbs.

Rather than keep a full-time embalmer on staff, funeral directors hired Dad when they had a "call." That way they saved money and Dad worked as much as he wanted, which was most of the time. Dad insisted that they call him whenever a body came in, even in the middle of the night—he didn't want his work to pile up—so our phone rang day and night. Dad taught me to answer the phone when I was a little kid, "He's not here right now; may I take a message?" Then I took a name, wrote it clearly in my best handwriting so Dad could read it later—Lynch and Sons, Kingsley, Sawyer, Cole, Spaulding, Sullivan, Fisher, Calhoun—and I repeated the phone number they gave me to be sure I heard it right.

We lived in apartments above the chapels in three funeral homes before I was six years old and I had to be quiet because people were grieving downstairs.

The "be quiet" rule was still in effect when I was five-and-a-half years old and we moved out of the last funeral home into a new house in Berkley, Michigan. I guess Dad just didn't like me talking no matter where we lived.

~~~

"Piggy-back!" he crouches down for me to climb on, I'm six years old, I shake my head knowing that he's headed into the lake over my head, no, you'll go under, no I won't, yes you will, no I won't I won't don't be such a baby, you'll go under, no, no, no, do you promise you won't go under, I promise, you really, *really* promise, I promise, so I climb onto his back and he carries me piggy-back into the lake riding on a promise that he won't go under, but he does—before I'm ready and can take a deep breath.

The weight of the water closes over my head—swallows me whole—the lake gulps me down, blue-green transparent—sunlight reaches faintly through the deep, silent water to touch me—and Dad keeps me under. I cling to his back, terrified to let go, I can't swim, and the shore is so far away; my lungs burn, his lungs are bigger than mine, he's a grownup, he can hold his breath longer than I can. I don't know how far away the surface is, how distant the shore, so I hold on. I hate that I need someone who betrayed me. I'm stunned, furious, broken. If I can't trust my own father, who can I trust?

~~~

Some years later, he tells me, "You're going to die not being able to breathe—"

I remember the lake (he resurfaced when it suited him); I can't imagine a worse death than being deprived of air.

"—because of your allergies," he specifies, "and I'm going to die of a heart attack. One day I'll go just like that." He snaps his fingers.

"How are Mom and the boys going to die?"

He thinks about it. "I don't know. And I don't know who's going to embalm you."

The thought of being embalmed horrifies me. I saw an embalming machine once—Dad had it in the car—and I smelled the sickening odor that wafted up from it.

It had a plastic container to hold the embalming fluid and a base with a motor, pump, and a hose. Incisions are made in an artery and embalming fluid is pumped in, which forces the blood out into a drain.

"I don't think I could embalm you," Dad says, "but I wouldn't want anyone else to do it. Oh well," he shrugs, "I'll probably die before you and I won't have to worry about it."

I'm immensely relieved. Yes, Dad, please die before me, please, I couldn't stand having you do that to me with all those hoses and nozzles and smelly liquids and sharp-pointed instruments.

~~~

Dad and I are getting ready to run errands, this time in the car instead of the hearse, which he saves for official business: picking up and delivering bodies and going on funerals.

I take a small cardboard box off the front seat as I slide in. It doesn't have any writing or markings on it. "What's this?"

He starts the car and we're off. "Do you know what 'cremains' are?"

Startled, I say, "Yes." Someone's ashes. There's a person in here, or there *was* a person, but the box is so small. It's a child. I place it carefully behind me on the backseat.

An ambulance siren breaks into my thoughts, Dad tracks it to a car accident. We sit at the side of the road and look at the pain and suffering. Dad slumps in his seat, lost in thought, studying the scene before us. A young man in black dress slacks and a white shirt stands by a wrecked car and looks shaken, a trickle of blood on his full, lower lip. He's handsome; my mind snaps a picture, snap, and one more for the memory "photo album," snap.

~~~

Dad finishes eating dinner before Mom, my brothers, and I do, and he pulls out the newspaper and reads the obituaries to us with commentary. "This little boy got himself killed because he ran out between parked cars; that's so stupid." Dad has a long, narrow face with a high hairline and a slight underbite that's more pronounced when he glares at me, "You better not do anything so stupid."

I try to ignore him and frown at the stewed tomatoes sitting in a bowl of watery, pink juice in front of me, and I wonder how many mouthfuls it'll take to finish before I can have the apple pie Mom made for dessert. We don't have dessert usually, but we have it—like a bribe or an apology—on the nights we have something I hate, like liver and onions, and stewed tomatoes; the worst dinner ever.

"I took care of him," Dad says and jabs the newspaper with his finger. "He died of tuberculosis like you're going to if you don't get outside and get some fresh air!"

I taught myself to type when I was nine. I prefer to stay inside to write my stories. The last time Dad told me I'd get TB if I didn't get some fresh air, I dragged a chair and card table outdoors and put the typewriter on it. He stood inside the house looking out at me; he seemed angry, as though he thought I was being a smart aleck. I was just trying to get him off my case and get some fresh air, so I wouldn't die not being able to breathe.

I'm not sure that Mom likes some of my stories. I showed her one, "The Case of the Sunburned Model," about a woman who's murdered by being drugged and left in the sun on a lawn chair, so she dies of dehydration and severe sunburn. The murderer wants it to look like she just fell asleep in the sun and it sucked the life out of her. It's a clever story and I'm proud of it.

Mom said, "Write about things you know. I like your animal stories and fairy stories." Yeah, like fairies are real. I wrote a 12-page story in the first grade (my handwriting was large, so the story wasn't "single-spaced," like typewritten) and the teacher had me read it to the class. When the prince swung down on a vine to rescue the princess, the kids laughed. It was a dramatic scene, and they laughed. It was humiliating. I haven't read anything in front of anyone since. Maybe they liked the story, but laughter wasn't the reaction I wanted.

Dad shakes out the newspaper and turns to the second page of obituaries. "This woman here was at Sawyer Funeral Home. She died because she was stupid and went to a doctor who made a stupid mistake and killed her." He fumes, "And this one, someone else did the work."

"The work" being the embalming. That was the "call" that got away. He works day and night. How much more can he handle? Maybe it was good that someone else got that job.

My brother, Bill, who's seven—three years younger than I am—jiggles his legs. Mom has him on yeast tablets for the Vitamin B to try to settle his nerves. My youngest brother, Matt, is still in a highchair and probably clueless at this point.

As Dad continues to read the obituaries out loud and comment on them, Mom quietly clears the plates and puts out the apple pie.

~~~

I swallowed more than dinner in those days. I ate fear and anger, and like food they became part of me, fueled my dreams, my creativity, and my anxiety. I swallowed what I wanted to tell Dad: stop, just stop with the obituaries and let me eat in peace or let me tell you what happened at school today and how I got a good report card; but all he wants is silence.

There were a lot of silences when I was growing up, and I did a lot of listening. It's amazing what I hear when I listen to silence. I hear the inner workings of things: the earth in its orbit, the slow rhythm of tides, and the crawl of the sea. I hear stars twinkling, the sun trailing the moon behind it, and the Breath behind my breath.

Sometimes it seems that I can hear people from the insides of their heads, the twisted tangle of their thoughts, their anguish, so loud that I think they spoke to me and I answer, and they say, "I didn't say anything, how'd you know what I was thinking?" And the color drains from their faces; I change the subject, flustered and embarrassed, and I'm even more afraid to speak the next time.

A college roommate tells me that she can see in the dark like a cat and feels like a freak because of it. With me it's hearing. I hear a faucet dripping a room away, the contraction of water pipes deep in the remote walls of the house, a clock ticking in another room, and once I tracked a tiny sound to the floor in a corner of my home office. A slug had crawled in under the door from outside, made its way down the hall, and was on one of my manuscripts nibbling the letters off a page of print.

I hear various parts of me whispering—the lost little girl crying for comfort, physicians conferring with each other and going about their healing, creativity asking for an invitation or an audience—the zip and zing of electricity in my brain.

A boyfriend in college says, "If you listen, you can hear your scars. Press a scar with a matchstick," he demonstrates on the scar on his forearm, "and you'll hear a change in the sound of silence."

The only scar I have is from when I was a baby walking on the couch; I fell against the windowsill and chomped down on my tongue; I don't want to probe that scar, so I take his word for it.

~~~

The places I've lived in the presence of death make me crave silence like a nutrient. And deep within that silence Something moves, a spirit, I feel it. I want to interpret that Spirit, explore the meaning and mystery of it, and live from within it. I hate anything loud that interrupts the silence: fireworks, blaring music, or piercing laughter. I carry earplugs everywhere I go, just in case, and slip them in when no one's looking.

Today I live in the country. My house is silent and solid as it sits on a ridge overlooking the lake. I stand in the entryway, look out at the water. I go into the living room with its dark paneling and high ceiling. The sun streams across hardwood floors. It's so quiet in here. Sometimes I spend days alone in the silent house, preferring it.

2. The Hour of Lead

This is the hour of lead, remembered, if outlived,
as freezing persons recollect the snow.
First—chill—then stupor—then the letting go.
— Emily Dickinson

I'm the only kid who goes out for bodies and ice cream. I like to go with Dad on pickups and deliveries because he doesn't call me an imbecile in public if I ask a question—like he does at home—and then we go out for ice cream. A hearse outside the Dairy Queen creates quite a stir. Add to the creepy effect the fact that Dad is big—230 pounds, 6-feet-6-inches tall—and has the somber look of a man who knows death up close and personally.

We haul death to and from hospitals, funeral homes, and airports, and I pretend it doesn't bother me, but I don't like the way people gawk at us when we drive by and some of them laugh when they see me. I'd rather Dad have another job. Lissa's dad is a barber. Lissa is my best friend. Diane is another good friend. Her dad sells Kenmore refrigerators and other large household appliances. Nicky and Jimmy's dad next door is a milkman. Then there are the kids who live in the big, brick houses in Huntington Woods. Their dads are said to be doctors and lawyers.

Today we're taking the hearse to pick up a body from Eastern Michigan Asylum for the Insane (also called Pontiac State Hospital). It's a self-contained town, an entire city unto itself with a church, a greenhouse, shops, a bakery, offices, cottages, wards, sleeping rooms for 3,100 patients, an infirmary, a dairy, and its own herd of cattle.

It's a short drive—about 10 miles—from our small home in the quiet suburbs, a nice ride into the country. And all too soon, there it is on the horizon, a huge complex of imposing gothic, brick buildings—like haunted mansions in the movies with endless rooms and Victorian spires and slate roofs, towers and turrets—growing larger and larger as we approach.

Eastern Michigan Asylum for the Insane, Pontiac, Michigan, c. 1876
https://commons.wikimedia.org/wiki/File:EasternMichiganAsylum.jpg

Dad pulls up to the front door of the main building and parks. You think we'd go to a side door or a back door, but no, we pull up right in front of the place in a hearse. That must really depress the inmates—or are they called residents or patients?

Dad says, "This place caught fire in the 1800s, the women's ward, before electricity when they used candlelight."

Imagine this vast, eerie place after dark, lit by candlelight: halls and rooms, narrow corridors, flickering shadows and attics, lock down. I just know it's haunted.

He adds, "Five-hundred women got loose. Some had to be kept from running back into the burning building."

I stare at the place and try to imagine fire peeling back the walls of their confinement—or their security—and they run wild and unpredictable across the dark lawns and empty acres that surround the place, they run against a background of flames.

Dad shakes his head, "They tried to run back in. That was so stupid."

No, Dad, not stupid, insane. I think there's a difference.

"There are children in there," he says. "They have their own ward."

I'm startled. Insanity is way too big for a child to contain. Madness should be an adult thing. How is it that children go insane enough to be put in a place like this? Could it happen to me? Do they have someone to tuck them in at night, read stories to them, love them, or are they alone and terrified like I feel on the outside?

Dad, wearing his customary dark suit, white shirt, tie, and black shoes, goes into the building and leaves me alone in the hearse.

It must be awful to die in there, to have an insane asylum be the last place you see. Do they give people shock treatments? It's terrifying to think that someone shoots electricity through your brain until you have seizures and forget for a moment—or forever—what was bothering you. I'm going to keep my thoughts and feelings to myself, bottled up inside and guarded, or someone might tell me that I'm crazy.

What if the insane people smell me out here—sense my shaky hold on reality—and, like zombies, lumber up to the hearse to study me? What if they surround me, their palms pressed against the windows, trying to get at me, their eyes vacant, yet trained on me, their pale, blue lips gently brushing the window as if to taste it, but leaving no warm, moist breath behind on the glass?

I'm so cold. If I were to go insane and lose control would someone warehouse me in a place like this until death released me? My eyes travel along the red brick walls of the first floor, move up to the second floor, third, and up there, on the top floor, a young man is hitting his forehead slowly against the bars of a narrow window. Does the hearse scare him, make sense to him, to look outside and see a young girl looking up at him, her face framed by the window of a funeral coach? Does he know who died, why we're here, or is he just trying to rock away his despair?

Who is Dad bringing out? Who found death the only escape, man, woman, or child? I'm afraid to ask, "Who is it?" too fragile to hear the answer.

3. Red Rover, Red Rover
A friend is a second self. — Author Unknown

I was seven years old, in second grade, and Lissa was five when her family moved into the neighborhood. Her mom asked my mom if I'd walk her to school. She had blue eyes and long, blonde hair and was wearing a pretty blouse and skirt and carrying a pencil box. She looked brave for her first day of kindergarten. Maybe she felt safe because she was with an older girl who'd protect her on the walk to Pattengill Elementary School, seven blocks away—half a mile.

I had two responsibilities: to feed Penny, my cocker spaniel, and Tico, my parakeet, and now, walk Lissa to school. If I didn't protect her, something bad might happen to her.

Dad warned me, "If you're not careful, if you're stupid, someone will hit you on the head and drag you into the bushes." He didn't say what would happen in there, but I was sure it'd be awful. I won't let anything like that happen to Lissa. I watch the bushes and shadows between the houses in case anyone jumps out to grab her. If that happens, I'll bite and scratch and tear him to pieces! And scream so people in the houses come to help.

We sleep over at each other's houses, suntan in our swimming suits in the backyard, and dress like gypsies on Halloween. We go to the lake and the zoo with our families and make sandwiches and eat them in the field across the street, Greenfield Road. Sometimes I pull a delicate, blue flower off a stem and lick the pollen out of the middle, and then Lissa does it, too—because I did.

~~~

I'm 11 now; Lissa's nine and we're playing in the vacant lot. I call, "Statues!" and kids come running from the nearby backyards: Lissa's sister Sandy, my brother Bill, and neighbors Dougie, Linda, Jimmy, and Mike. Four-year-old Pookie clumps over in his mom's high heels and sits on the sidelines on a large flat rock. He's wearing a t-shirt, shorts, a pearl necklace, and white gloves and has a large purse slung over his shoulder.

I'm older than the other kids and like being in charge, unlike at home where I can't control much of anything. In "Statues" I spin each kid around and around and let go. They fly away from me and land in all sorts of silly positions. I ask them what they are—horses, dogs, dancers, etc.—and then they have to chase me in those positions. They look so funny trying to catch me, especially Jimmy who fell on his side and can't move very well, but then they all circle me at same time and block my escape. Lissa tackles me, and then she gets to be "It."

She spins us around, lets us go, and asks me, "What are you?"

"An airplane," I say from my seated position on the ground.

Dougie is a house painter, Sandy an eagle, Linda a racecar, Mike a football player, and Jimmy a wrestler.

"Go!" Lissa shouts and we chase her. I leap off the ground and swoop at her so fast she doesn't have time to think, and I tag her.

"Hey, that's cheating," Dougie protests, "You have to stay in the same position."

"*Nuh-uh*, I'm an airplane and airplanes fly. I was sitting on the runway, and then I took off. I'm still an airplane whether I'm on the runway or in the air."

The game disintegrates. Sandy and Jimmy debate whether I cheated and, excited by the chaos, Dougie shoves Linda. Sitting on the sidelines, Pookie adjusts his pearl necklace and seems to disapprove of all of us.

"You cheated," Dougie pouts.

Indignant, "I did not. I was being creative."

Weepy now, "You cheated."

"Do over," Jimmy calls out cheerfully. I sigh, aggravated. He wants to start the game over from just before the disputed play, so we can keep playing rather than have people go away angry. A do-over would make them feel better but would cancel my win. I won by being smart and I won't let anyone undo my win.

"Nope, no do-over," I say emphatically. "Let's play something else. Red Rover."

They're still pouting and complaining as we form two lines facing each other some distance apart. I'm in line with Sandy, Bill, and Mike opposite Lissa, Dougie, Linda, and Jimmy.

I whisper to Sandy and Bill on each side of me, "Hold wrists instead of hands; it makes the line stronger." I narrow my eyes, scrutinize the other team: Jimmy is little and won't be able to break our chain, so we'll get to keep him and make our line longer. "Red Rover, Red Rover, send Jimmy over."

He comes running as fast as he can and leaps, folding himself in half over our gripped wrists. He can't break through and joins our line.

Next, Linda calls me over. I charge toward her and Dougie to make it look like I'm running straight toward their link, then veer off course suddenly and hurl myself against Linda and Lissa's hands because they let their guard down—and I break them apart. They rub their hands, "*Owww!*"

Dougie's eyes widen, "You cheated again. You tricked us."

"I did not. I was just being clever. You're not any fun to play with," I scold, furious at being called a cheater again.

Pookie left. He watches us play until he gets bored—or scared if we argue—and then drifts away to go do whatever he thinks is more important. He always seems to be on his way to somewhere else.

"Oh, I give up," I say, incensed at being wrongfully accused of cheating. "I'm going home to write." In my stories, I'm totally in control. People do whatever I tell them. I can make them win or lose—heck, I don't even have to make them human.

~~~

Lissa and I tromp down the sidewalk, arm in arm, making sure that we each start with the same foot, so we'll be in step all the way to wherever we're going: right foot, left foot, right, left, right.

"Let's go to the store and see if the guys are there," I say. They're stock boys who work at National Grocery store across the street and are probably in high school. I go to Anderson Junior High; Lissa still goes to Pattengill Elementary.

Halfway there we cross paths with some boys on the sidewalk, she pushes me between them and her, and then pinches my arm real hard. I hiss, "*Owww*, stop it. Quit pinching me. You're just drawing attention to yourself."

She gives my arm another pinch for good measure. "I want attention, except boys are our worst enemies. The ones I see coming out of Anderson Junior High are creeps. I bet they all are."

Hmmm, there's something more to boys than she realizes. There's just something about them.

The Ouija Board says that the stock boys' names are Jerry and Gary. Ouija says that Jerry likes Lissa and Gary likes me, and it says that I'm going to marry someone named Chuck and have five kids; Lissa's going to get married, too, and have three. I hope our families visit each other when we're grown up. It gives me a funny feeling to think of having a husband.

~~~

Lissa and I kept in touch occasionally when I went away to college. I made new friends and had my first boyfriend. Lissa made new friends, too, and was "discovered" walking down the street by the director of a modeling agency, and it wasn't a scam. She was slim, tall, and beautiful with blonde hair. They sent her on assignments, but some were in Detroit and she got nervous going there by herself. She had anxiety attacks and stopped accepting jobs.

Being two years older than Lissa, I figured I'd do everything before she did: wear a bra, get my period, go to college, get married, have kids (five according to the Ouija board). Turns out I went to college and she didn't. She got married, had a son, and got divorced and married again. I chose not to marry or have kids, so maybe Lissa caught up with me and, in some ways, passed me.

I drive up to a large, elegant home on a lake in an exclusive neighborhood. Lissa opens the door, throws her arms around me, and draws me into her home. She's crying, so happy to see me. I hug her tightly. We're the same height now. Her home is beautiful. She's quite artistic and has a wonderful sense of color and style. We visit as though we saw each other just yesterday and we talk for hours.

She bakes chicken and vegetables for dinner, and her husband, Ray, joins us. I like him. He's attentive, friendly, and smart. At dinner, the three of us share our most embarrassing experiences and I laugh so hard that my nose starts to run; an allergy attack.

Ray leaves after dinner. Lissa and I continue to visit and make up for all the years we missed. I remind her of playing in the vacant lot.

"I ate Morning Glories because you did," she stated.

"Those weren't Morning Glories," I say, horrified. "Morning Glories are poisonous. They were Chicory. And we didn't eat them. We just licked the pollen out of the middle."

"But they might have been poisonous," she says uneasily.

"But they weren't. Chicory is safe to eat. They use it in coffee in New Orleans to bring people good luck and remove curses. I think my family was cursed; they were weird. Dad and I went to the asylum in Pontiac to pick up a body; it was very traumatic."

"I know. I was with you."

Her words jolt me. I frown, "No, I was alone."

"There was a man hitting his forehead on the bars of a window on the top floor."

She saw him, too. A cold, sinking feeling tells me it's true. She was with me. How could I not remember something so important?

She says, "I was afraid of going crazy after that. That was one of the things that contributed to my anxiety."

The trip with my dad in the hearse was part of the reason she developed an anxiety disorder and suffered panic attacks that plagued her much of her life and ended her modeling career. My head feels cottony inside. The world is far away. I was supposed to protect her. It was my responsibility.

"We might have gone there more than once," she adds.

I shake my head. I only remember once. Was I repressing the other times? Something inside me feels frantic like a bird trying to escape, flapping its wings against the bars of a cage.

"Those rides to Pontiac State Hospital were quite unsettling for me as a youngster," she says, and then, "I'm sure your dad didn't realize how they would affect us."

Yes, how could he have known?

You were entrusted to me at an early age; I should have protected you, but how? I thought I was alone in the hearse, when in fact, you were with me; I was with my best friend.

~~~

Lissa and I say good night. I make myself comfortable in her cozy guestroom. I spared her the grisly details—which I learned years later—about Pontiac State Hospital. What started out in 1878, as a humanitarian project to house the homeless and mentally ill, devolved into a place where a doctor, in 1913, conducted inhumane experiments on "mentally defective" patients. He was a dermatologist and "syphilologist," not a surgeon. He used a dental drill on the skulls of living patients to extract syphilitic brain tissue to study. With 3,100 patients, they had an abundance of research subjects to use for whatever.

In the 1920s, "eugenics" was an accepted practice. Eugenics was the science of "improving" the human race by controlling reproduction in order to increase desirable, heritable characteristics. It was common for surgeons to sterilize people whom they deemed to be "feeble-minded imbeciles."

Michigan was one of the states that aggressively sterilized people considered "inferior" due to low intelligence, anti-social behavior, and "insanity."

That place was more than spooky. I must have sensed the agony that emanated from it. And the man hitting his forehead on the bars, what had he seen, what had he endured?

I shiver off the terrifying thoughts. The property was sold to developers eventually, the buildings demolished in stages and all gone by the year 2000. If only it were that easy to dismantle a nightmare.

The grounds returned to open fields for a while, like my vacant lot only much larger, where children—brothers, sisters, and neighbors—must have played until developers built houses.

I played strategically when I was young, and still do. I was smart and fast. I had to win, and I had to be right. Dad told me that stupid people die and sometimes children end up in insane asylums.

I close my eyes. Breathe in deeply and out slowly. Travel back in time to revisit a memory.

It's quiet, early evening. Mothers cook dinners, fathers come home from work, and the traffic thins out along Greenfield Road. I'm young again, and children move—shadows and silhouettes—

playing in the vacant lot where I resisted the rules of the game or changed games entirely on a whim to control the play.

The fragrant breeze is gentle, whispery, and easy with us. Chicory grows along the fence. There's a bright new moon in the sky and fireflies in the bushes.

I change the memory a little. I tell Bill and Sandy, standing on each side of me in line, "Just hold hands this time, not wrists," and they protest, "But you told us that holding wrists makes the line stronger!"

"Just the same, let's hold hands," and then I call out, "Red Rover, Red Rover, send Lissa over."

She comes running toward me in the twilight, her blonde hair unfurling behind her, my best friend whom I tried to protect but couldn't save from a ride in a hearse to an insane asylum. Oh, my first and forever friend, I'm sorry.

Her feet gain traction in the grass, she barrels toward our line, throws her full weight against our clasped hands, and I loosen my grip so she can break my hold.

4. Muck Fires and Farm Boys

There would be no advantage to be gained by
sowing a field if the harvest did not return
more than was sown. — Napoleon Hill

Every summer we make a pilgrimage to Harrison's farm in southern Michigan, where they grow onions, cabbage, corn, potatoes, carrots, and mint. Vegetables thrive in the "muck," the rich, porous soil, which is made mostly from dead plant material.

The Harrison kids call their parents by their first names, Harold and Rhonda, which amazes me and earns Mom's disapproval, "Children should call their parents 'Mother' and 'Father,' or 'Mom' and 'Dad.'" She also insists that I call her parents "Grandfather" and "Grandmother." I can call Dad's parents "Grandma" and "Grandpa," but not hers.

Harrison's live in a ranch-style house with a big clothes washer and dryer, no rugs on the floors so they can be mopped frequently, a Golden Retriever named Thurby, and barn swallows nesting over the back door. Harold and Rhonda have five kids—a girl, Jan, and four boys—who work the farm with them and track in loads of dirt on their clothes and shoes, so they have to wash clothes every day.

I liked Alex, the oldest boy, ever since I met him when I was four years old and he was five, but I only see him once a year for about a week because they live 100 miles from us. Last year when I was 13, I wrote in my diary:

> For an English assignment, Alex had to write a letter to someone explaining a sport. He wrote to me explaining basketball, which he likes to play. He was thinking of me! A long time ago he said that I was his girlfriend. Is it possible that a boy can like a girl for so long? I wish our families got together more often.

Sometimes I dream that he kisses me. Lissa asked what I would do if he really did kiss me. I told her I'd kiss him right back; nothing like playing hard to get. Ha! I don't know what I'd do.

Boys at school wink at me and joke with me—I don't joke back because I don't know what to say. I go ice skating with Bob from school who seems to like me, but he's never kissed me.

I'm afraid to like a guy and have him like me. If a guy shows an interest, I don't respond. Mom says maybe it's because she doesn't respond to Dad in a positive way (they fight a lot). They set a bad example and Mom knows it. I'm confused. I don't know what to do.

Dad treats me like an adult now. He does this by telling me dirty jokes. I understand them, but I don't laugh or encourage him.

~~~

We arrive at the Harrison farm in the late afternoon. Harold tells me, "Alex is distilling mint, I put him in charge," and laughs. "He really cracks the whip if the workers don't do it right."

I'm in awe. Alex is 14 years old, a year older than I am. Imagine ordering people around when you're just a teenager, they have to do what you say, and your dad admires you for it.

On the way to the distillery Jan tells me how Alex has changed. "He drives, shaves, wears size 13 shoes, is six-feet-one-inch tall, and popular at school." I look hopeful for what I really want to know. She continues, "He told me he has a girlfriend. I asked if she lives in town and he said no. I asked, in Lansing? He said he didn't know anyone in Lansing. Then I asked, Detroit? And he said near there."

I'm beaming inside. We live 12 miles north of Detroit.

Alex flashes a big smile at me from atop the distillery platform. He's so cute: blond hair, brown eyes, confident. It's good he's up there and I'm down here because I can't think of anything to say to him. I might say something stupid. I'm so clueless around boys.

There's a flurry of activity. Chopped mint was brought in from the fields in large wagons; each wagon holds about two tons. The workers force high-pressure steam through the mint into distillation tubs and the oily steam rises and is routed into smaller barrels where the oil rises to the top of the water, is drained, and stored in steel drums for sale. It takes about an hour and a half to distill one load. There's a spigot with a drop of clear liquid on the end. One of the boys invites me to try it, so I catch a drop on my finger and lick it off, surprised at the burning intensity. Jan assures me, "It'll be diluted before it's used in chewing gum, ice cream, and desserts."

The next morning Alex appears at breakfast wearing a gas mask. He already ate and is on his way to spread chicken manure. "It smells really bad," he laughs as he heads out the door. And so it goes throughout our visit. I see him on his way to and from the fields. Harold gave him several acres to farm. This afternoon Harold went into town and left Alex, who's 14, in charge of the hired help. Within the hour, Alex fired one of the workers. He fired an adult. That's mind-boggling. At home my chores amount to taking turns with my brother Bill washing or drying the dishes. Alex farms acres of land, oversees the distillery, and supervises adults.

After breakfast we go out to the onion field, Jan hands me a heavy pair of shears, and I drop to my knees in the muck next to an empty wooden crate. We begin to "top" onions alongside the migrant workers. The sun warms the muck; the pungent odor is heavenly. There are some cute guys in the fields. One, Jimmy, laughs at Jan and me as he drives by on the tractor tossing empty crates along the rows for us to fill. I pull up a clump of onions and cut off the tops; they bounce into the crate.

The migrant workers, who started behind us in the parallel rows, pass us and are way ahead. Jan and I topped 18 crates, made 90¢ apiece, and I cut my fingers three times. The blades get slick with juice, which stings in a cut, but the heat and muck relax me; my cheeks are flushed, hair's a mess. Jan suggests a swim at the gravel pit, and we find Alex there.

The water is deep, dark, and so chilly that I gasp for breath; I ease into it. Jan whispers, "Alex's watching you." I close my eyes and imagine I'm swimming through the sky. I'm graceful, aware of the slim length of my body in the fluid, buoyant water. I climb out and dry off. Alex comes over and stands in front of me. He reaches a finger slowly toward my breast, stops short of it, I watch, mesmerized. He pulls his hand away and we go back to the house.

Harrisons are Christian Scientists. All I know about Christian Scientists is they don't believe in doctors. Harold says, "If our faith isn't strong enough to heal us or our children, we'll go to a doctor."

They talk with Mom about it. She likes to think about God. She told me, "One day you'll realize that God is within you, and you'll feel close to him whenever you remember that and turn within. It doesn't happen to everyone."

I think she's saying that *she* feels close to God. I'm glad that something comforts her because she doesn't seem happy with Dad.

I want to learn about Christian Science, but right now it's more important to ride into town with Alex, Jan, Jimmy from the field, and a couple other boys. This town only has a few hundred residents, nothing exciting going on, so we're going to Albion, which is bigger. I don't get a chance like this every day. God will have to wait.

We pile into the car and stop on our way to Albion to steal apples from an orchard. I follow the boys to the fence and climb over. How far away is the farmhouse? Can anyone see us? What if farm dogs attack us? My heart's racing, I snatch an apple off a tree and run back to the fence. I scramble over it, run to the car, and ride breathlessly into town with the farm kids. I've never stolen anything ever. It takes me quite a while to calm down.

In Albion, we cruise the streets and get into trouble, which means smoking cigarettes and gawking at other kids who are also smoking and cruising. Every now and then one of the boys gets out of the car and goes to talk to someone in another car. Stealing apples, smoking part of a cigarette—I put it out in the ashtray when no one was looking—cruising unsupervised with no curfew; I'm giddy with the excitement of how bad I'm being.

On the way home, the headlights flash briefly on a wisp of smoke curling lazily from a field. "Muck fire," one of the boys says and sniffs, "That smell stays with you. You remember it forever."

Like embalming fluid; whenever I think about it, I can smell it again, distinctive, a little like I'd imagine a gangrene-soaked, wet bandage would smell on a hot, humid day.

"How does a fire start?" I ask.

"Lightning, a spark from a passing train, or a cigarette tossed out of a car window," Alex answers.

"A muck fire's a bitch to fight," Jimmy adds. "It can burn for months, sometimes years. It spreads underground so you don't know where it is. You can't use heavy equipment to fight it because the ground under it might collapse."

"Doesn't it need air to burn?" I ask.

"Muck is porous. There are plenty of oxygen pockets to keep a fire going, even underground. A field looks solid, but there's fire underneath."

Alex adds, "You don't know where the boundaries are. One fire burned 15,000 acres underground as far as we could tell. It can take months of rain—or millions of gallons of water hauled in—to flood the muck, but just when you think you've put out a fire it starts up again somewhere else. It can destroy a tree's roots a mile away, so the tree suddenly falls over on someone."

Wow. You don't know there's a fire there and suddenly a tree falls on you. How do you put out a fire you don't see and can't find?

~~~

I write an essay "The Onion Field" about topping onions with the migrant workers and how it was an adventure for me, a "city" kid, but a way of life for them. I send it to the Scholastic Writing Awards contest, and I'm thrilled when it wins Honorable Mention.

Sometimes I think about the muck fire. There's something sinister about hidden things, a fire below with no discernible boundaries that can burn quietly for years and then surprise us suddenly and so terribly.

Little did I know at the time, there was an unseen "fire" burning underground in my life.

5. Hernias and Hearses

It's no use reminding yourself daily that you are mortal:
it will be brought home to you soon enough.
— Albert Camus

When we lived in the funeral home, if the chapel downstairs was full, Dad would bring a fully loaded casket up into our apartment and we used it as a coffee table (I might have had milk and cookies on top of someone's grandma). He was forever bringing death home—figuratively or literally—and setting it right down in the middle of my life.

I can't believe that they didn't have somewhere downstairs where they could store it until the funeral, and I concluded that the casket in the living room was for my education. It emphasized something Dad wanted to teach me: "If you aren't really careful, and do something stupid, you'll get yourself killed and end up in a coffin like this." His fear came out as anger. He raged at me for no apparent reason other than his own unhappiness—that, and maybe, he couldn't forgive me for being mortal.

He told me frequently, "People are stupid, and people who die are stupid," and then he called me stupid. I didn't understand; if I was stupid, and stupid people died, why was I still alive? Maybe I had a quota of mistakes—a great cosmic quota—that I was allowed before I made the big one, the final one. Trouble was I didn't know what the quota was. I was terrified of messing up and became a perfectionist to ward off the grim reaper. I got as smart as I could and proved it by getting awards and honors in school, making good grades and, eventually, earning two master's degrees.

I obsessed: what if I die and people find the first draft of a story or a book on my computer and think that's the best I could do? I

The Mortician's Child

picture them shaking their heads sadly, "She really went downhill toward the end. Whatever happened to her talent?"

~~~

Well, Dad got a hernia from too much heavy lifting and had an operation, so when he asked me to go with him on a delivery, this time from Detroit to Chicago, he said, "You might have to drive some of the way if I get tired."

Yeah, like that'll happen. I'm 16, and it's illegal for me to drive. I haven't even taken Driver's Education in school yet or been behind the wheel of anything, so I sit back in the plush seat and, expecting a relaxed trip, entertain myself by counting the number of semi-trucks that pass us—one about every three minutes. The scenery rolls by— the hills green with recent rains—pleasant, fresh, and hypnotic.

He breaks into my thoughts, "After my hernia operation the nurse asked if I knew where I was, and I told her 'the funeral home.' It gave her quite a start. Your mother explained that I work in a funeral home."

I smile. Encouraged by my smile, he smiles, too, and reminisces, "I was leading a funeral procession once. They go about 15 miles an hour on side streets, but I started to think about something else and drove faster and faster, and when I looked in the rearview mirror they weren't anywhere in sight. I'd lost them."

I laugh. A funeral procession is supposed to be a dignified, solemn caravan of mourners following a hearse from the funeral service to the cemetery; it's funny to imagine them trying to keep up with the hearse.

He pulls onto the shoulder of the highway and turns off the engine. "I'm tired, you drive for a while."

I'm shocked. *But, but I, I don't know how*. Doesn't he know that I've never had a driving lesson?

He gets out of the hearse, goes around the front end of it to my side, and opens the door. Stunned, stiff-legged, I get out and walk slowly to the driver's side—it's a very long walk—I can't believe this is happening. This is a 7,000-pound funeral coach, this is a freeway, and I've never had a driving lesson!

I slip into the roomy seat behind the wheel, notice the smell of carnations, slide the seat forward, turn the key in the ignition, look over my shoulder to make sure the lane is clear, and pull out onto the busy freeway during rush hour.

I white knuckle it, dizzy and terrified, for more than an hour. Something buzzes deep inside my ears. Can I control this thing, keep it on the road, keep up with traffic?

What if someone changes lanes without warning or slams on their brakes in front of me? I wouldn't know what to do.

What if I pass out, faint, lose control?

What if I cause an accident?

What if I kill us?

A riddle: a vehicle carrying three people goes over a cliff, all three are dead at the scene, but the newspapers report that only two were killed in the crash. Is this faulty reporting? Answer: No, it's not. One of the people was already dead. The vehicle was a hearse and the two passengers, a mortician and his daughter, were transporting a body to Chicago.

The bright sun glints off the slanted back windows of the cars ahead of me and nearly blinds me—it's nauseating, I don't have sunglasses, and the cars are all going fast, so terribly fast. A car with two guys speeds past us, they look over at me driving and laugh.

Rubber tires hum along the road, the hills zoom by, we pass exit after exit after exit.

What if I forget how to steer or can't stop?

What if I forget which side of the road I'm supposed to be on?

What if I forget everything?

Dad's asleep, head thrown back, mouth wide open, snoring. What a sight we must be, a traumatized young girl driving a hearse on a busy freeway with a "dead" man propped up in the front seat beside her.

6. Merry Christmas

Physical strength is measured by what we can carry; spiritual strength by what we can bear. — Author Unknown

I love Christmas lights, the large, clunky ones that are painted red, blue, green, and yellow. They don't do anything fancy like blink off and on, bubble or twinkle, or "chase" each other around the tree. They just nestle there in the branches, glow softly, and keep the darkness away with color, and if the paint gets chipped a little, I can look through the tiny window and see the light inside.

When I was four, I was afraid of Santa Claus. I told Mom, "I don't want a man in a red suit walking through the house at night." She assured me, "Santa represents love. Your dad and I bring you presents—in the spirit of giving—we're Santa Claus."

I'm so glad that she explained it and didn't lie to me by simply telling me not to worry because Santa is friendly.

~~~

All Dad wants every Christmas is socks and chocolate-covered cherries and, occasionally, a tie. It's like he has everything he needs, doesn't want us to go to any trouble, or is trying to save us money. I always feel like I should give him something more.

This Christmas he had to work. He's not here when I wake up and he comes home after I'm in bed.

The next day he and I sit alone at the kitchen table. He looks exhausted and depressed, "It was a family of seven."

That's why he was gone so long. It takes about two hours to embalm a body, so seven would take 14 hours, and he'd have to stop for lunch and dinner and, I'd think, to catch his breath in between, and maybe steady his nerves. It'd be just him—and them—alone in the embalming room, all day long and into the night.

I shift uneasily in my chair. Is he about to make me his confidant? I'm afraid that the only thing I'll be able to do for him is quietly shoulder the weight—the burden—of what he tells me.

He sighs, his breath ragged, "The father killed them with a double-bladed ax and then shot himself. They were covered with sheets when I got there. I didn't look at them all at once. I uncovered them one at a time when I was ready to start work." He pauses, continues, "There were ax marks on the little boy's arm as he held it in front of his face trying to protect himself."

I can't imagine how much blood there must have been from *seven* people. A terrible awareness settles into my bones, the realization that some parents kill their children and kill each other and kill themselves. And this father did it up close, not from a distance with a gun although he used one on himself; it's like he wanted to be close to each of them while he was doing it, and it must have taken a while.

Dad and I sit silently, him with his thoughts and me imagining, overcome with the horror of it. I mourn for the little boy who didn't know that his dad was going to slaughter him on Christmas. There would have been shock and heat and moisture—sweat and blood and tears—and everything in the house slick and slippery, the floors, walls, ax handle and blade, and a smell like copper; pennies held in a hot, sweaty fist.

What terror the little boy must have felt when he realized this was no reprimand from which he'd escape or recover. His father meant business, the ax hacking through his small body soft like cheese, bones like kindling, *oh, no, Daddy, no, oh don't, no, it hurts, it hurts so bad, why are you doing this, please don't, no, no, nooo.*

> And Jesus said, "Suffer the little children to come unto me and forbid them not, for such is the

kingdom of Heaven …" And he took them up in his arms, put his hands upon them, and blessed them.

His dad chopped him up like a cord of wood on Christmas morning. The Bible stories in my books do not comfort me! The songs do *not* comfort me:

Jesus loves me this I know for the Bible tells me so.
Little children to him belong, they are weak, but he
is strong.

The man hacked his babies to death and left the mess for my dad to clean up when he should have been at home watching me open my presents. Why does Jesus get to be strong and I don't? I will *not* be weak while someone else is strong!

Where was I while the killing was taking place? Maybe as I stirred in bed, my thoughts on presents, or maybe while I dressed by the heating vent in the bathroom. The man must have stalked the remainder of his family about the time I was doing something insignificant like eating soft-boiled eggs and toast. I'll never eat soft-boiled eggs again as a tribute to that little boy. And while I opened my presents, and pulled back the crisp, colorful wrapping paper tied with beautiful, bright ribbons, Dad stood in the gloom above the dead family and pulled back the sheets one by one.

Why am I alive and that little boy isn't? I see people interviewed on TV who survived disasters, airline crashes, earthquakes, and tornados—while others died—and they say that maybe they were spared because there was something God still wanted them to do. Is there something I'm meant to do, but what about the little boy whose life was full of potential; it doesn't make sense that there wasn't anything left for him to do or accomplish.

Survivors say piously, "Angels were watching over us, God had a hand in our survival." Where were the angels for the people crushed, burned, suffocated, or drowned? Where was God *seconds before* the winds, the flames, the tsunami?

The governor of the state tells the TV cameras, "Any loss of life is tragic, but only four people died in the tornado. God is good. He's watching out for us." The people behind her nod reverently.

~~~

Death rolls by Dad—slowly on an assembly line—he lifts the bodies off the "conveyor belt": this one died of cancer, this one of murder, this one by his own hand. Here's a little boy, little girl, a housewife, businessman, all dead. Death is so inventive, or maybe it isn't even a thing itself, but a by-product of the way we live our lives, a ghastly human invention. And the trick is to learn how to live a "perfect" life, whatever that is, to be so good that death comes mercifully in our sleep rather than in some gristly way.

I've been going to church every Sunday *for years* and to Youth Group almost every Wednesday night except when I have a migraine, which is frequently. And I'm taking "Communicants Class" to prepare me to join the church, but I am prepared for *nothing*.

Dad's stories scare me, how easy it is to die, and I find refuge in the stories that Mom reads to me and I escape in the stories I make up.

Mom had postpartum depression. We lived near Harold and Rhonda at the time. Harold told me later that, "Your mom sat for weeks in the rocking chair, holding you, and crying. Your dad was so worried that he asked us if there was anything we could do to help. That's how we became friends with your mom."

What affect did her tears, that sad "lullaby," have on my newly minted psyche? Did I imprint on sorrow?

Years later a friend tells me, "But she was holding you and rocking you. You didn't know that sobbing was a bad thing. You only knew that you were being held and tended to. She didn't hurt you or abandon you. She was rocking you and keeping you safe. It might have been a positive experience for you."

That's a fascinating thought, but if I stood next to people who heard real lullabies when they were babies, would you see something different in my eyes? Did the out-of-kilter hormones that percolated through Mom's body before I was born also rage through mine, did I bring some with me when she pushed me out of her and away?

She suffered through the depression without any medical help, sought escape in fantasy, and read me stories populated with witches, kings, and queens, stories that were about "good" that was absolute and "evil" that was equally so. We huddled together on the couch by the lamp and she read me my favorite story night after night, at my insistence, about a bunny with a magic nose who could turn the other animals pink or blue and did so with great delight—until one day he fell, bumped his nose, and accidentally turned himself pink from head to toe.

The bunny promised to be nicer to the other animals and they helped him wash himself off in the lake, but wouldn't you know, he forgot to wash the insides of his ears and to this day all bunnies have pink ears. The bunny carries the reminder of his mistake the rest of his life, as do all bunnies. The sins of the fathers visited on the sons and daughters even if the fathers repented? I don't deserve to inherit anyone's sin. Why do I need to atone for someone else? And the lesson of the bunny carried forward: use your magic for good or don't use it at all?

I want to be magic. I'm desperate to transcend this life with all its problems. I need to believe it's possible to bend the laws of physics and that I can do it.

~~~

    I pal around with Deena in high school (Lissa is still in junior high). Deena believes that babies are born bad and in need of redemption, and she knows just the "man" for the job. If people don't accept Jesus Christ as their Lord and Savior, God will send them straight to hell for eternity. But if God loves us unconditionally and gives people free will, why does he send us to hell if we choose "wrong"?

    I sleep over at Deena's house occasionally, but I like sleepovers at Lissa's better (her dad grills steaks and makes the best peanut-butter fudge). Deena shows me a painting, "The Garden of Earthly Delights" by an artist named Bosch. There are three panels in the painting: paradise, a place somewhere between paradise and hell, and then, of course, hell where people are suffering terribly; one naked guy has an arrow up his butt and he's climbing a ladder in spite of it. If that were me, I'd pull the arrow out, but maybe that's the point. If God wants an arrow there, it stays there, no matter what you try to do—and it's there forever. Deena dwells on the hell panel of the painting and chuckles softly to herself like she's enjoying it, like it excites her. I think all three panels are ghastly. There's way too much going on in them and the people don't look real. I don't even like the paradise panel.

    I don't believe that people are born sinners. I think that maybe we're born good and innocent like the little boy whose dad murdered him. If he hadn't been baptized or accepted Jesus yet, because he was too young to understand, or his parents were of a different faith, would he burn in hell forever—in addition to the agony of having been murdered? That's too cruel and senseless. Or maybe we're just born, and in need of inspiration and guidance (maybe Jesus could help with that).

~~~

As an adult, Deena is unwavering; she knows that her religion is right: one size fits all—case closed. She marries her high school sweetheart, has two children, and lives for decades in the same area where she grew up. I didn't want children, never married officially (I'm in a long-term relationship), lived in three different states, traveled extensively, and had three careers (writing, teaching, and speaking). I wrote two bestsellers and a time-management column for *Success* magazine and was "on the road" as a professional speaker when only two percent of business travelers were women.

Sometimes I envied Deena's safe, predictable life that seemed so manageable. Mine, on the other hand, was chaotic and messy; I never told her how difficult it was at my house. Years later she said, "Your dad always appeared to be very supportive of you and your brothers."

She and I experience everything differently. She sees Dad as supportive; I see him as a frequently angry, tormented man who embalmed a family gruesomely murdered and was so disturbed by it that he had to tell someone, and that was me, his 11-year-old daughter. Deena and I don't perceive life in general the exact same way (no two people ever do), so how can we possibly perceive God (whom no one has ever seen) exactly alike? I suspect there's an Absolute, but we each worship—or relate to it—differently. And yet Deena insists that I experience the same religious feelings that she does, use the same words to describe God, and practice the same rituals to worship God, and if I don't, she judges me by her own standards to my detriment; I'm going to hell. That doesn't make any sense to me.

We went to the same school, took many of the same classes, and played clarinet in the band; but she didn't know how precarious my life was on the inside, and that my spirituality was very hard won and precious to me, and that in the end, I'd come to believe that we each have the god we need.

~~~

Years later I realize that as I was growing up, I was suspended between the gruesome and the impossible, lost somewhere in between, emotionally missing, trying to find my feelings and the words to express them.

I ask Mom, "Did Dad ever tell you about his more difficult cases?"

"What do you mean?"

"The circumstances, how people died, like the Christmas he embalmed a whole family. The father killed his wife and kids with an ax and then shot himself."

She thinks for a minute, and then, "No, I think I'd remember something like that."

7. Snarl

That they may have a little peace, even the best dogs are compelled to snarl occasionally. — William Feather

Dad is bellowing at one of my brothers, "I'll tear your arm off and beat you with it!" It's hard to imagine what either of them did to warrant a threat like that.

Dad is having one of his meltdowns. He seems powerless and ineffective when he yells, like he thinks no one will listen to him if he speaks respectfully, but all he really does is make me go silent and go away. Never knowing what will set him off, I avoid him, lose myself in my writing, walk in the field across the street, and spend time alone in my room.

I go into the bathroom, turn on the fan so I can't hear the yelling, and sit on the edge of the bathtub. What a gruesome thing Dad said. Imagine having one of your own arms torn off and used against you like that. I feel like gagging. Dad would threaten to hurt his son and also make him an accomplice in his own injury.

~~~

My brother Bill and I used to be closer. When he was a baby, I'd cuddle him and murmur, "Sweetest little guy in the whole wide world." When he was older and invited too many friends to his birthday party (an afternoon at the roller rink), there wasn't room in the car for me, so he offered me his seat and was willing to stay home from his own party. And he reminds me that when I only made 90 cents topping onions on Harrison's farm, he made more than that and shared some of what he made with me. But we grew apart. Matt was born and both boys started to bully me relentlessly—they rifled through my desk and storage box in the attic, Bill violated my privacy by reading my diary, Matt called me names—and Dad and Mom's marriage began to crumble. We were a family in crisis.

The Mortician's Child

~~~

Dad tells me about another case. A young man shut the garage door and ran a hose from the tailpipe of his car to the inside of the car and turned the motor on. "He wrote about how it felt to die while he was dying. He didn't write a note to anyone in particular."

The man was methodic and scientific; studying himself as his life drained away, or maybe studying life in general and the process it goes through as it slips out of the body.

Dad's called when it's too late to help the living. He belongs to service clubs—the Kiwanis, Rotary, and Lions Club. I thought it was because he wanted to keep a high profile in the community, so people knew to call *him* when someone died. Could it also have been an attempt to contribute something to the living?

He can't go to work, feed us, or pay the bills unless someone dies. He doesn't visit people in the hospital because he doesn't want to appear eager. He sees people grieving every day, sees murdered children. His emotions must be all tangled up, snarled and snarling.

Did he want to rage at the young man who killed himself or the people who did stupid things and died, rage for the waste of life and pointless deaths, rage at not being able to do anything about it? Is that why he yells at Mom and us and calls us names? We're handy.

The background noise—like a persistent, low-grade fever—is Mom and Dad arguing, a soundscape of anger, desperation, and misery, and my brothers picking on me and taunting me without mercy, maybe because they can't get at the source, they can't tell Mom and Dad to either work it out between them or just be quiet. I carry a tremendous weight, a great cargo of sadness to and from school and church and friends' houses. I write in my diary (15 years old):

> I was in the bathroom brushing my hair when Bill came
> in and threw a towel over my head to tease me, so I

slapped him. He burst out crying. I never tell Mom how both of them tease me, they always do. I never tell her what I go through. I take their teasing and I'm crying inside. I don't have anyone in whom to confide.

I took the iodine bottle out of the medicine cabinet and stared at it. I smelled it. Apparently, a small amount of iodine in the diet is healthy but drinking a whole bottle will poison you. I don't know why I even think such things. I'm afraid that I'll get to the point where I'll automatically, suddenly without thinking, my hand will cause me to drink all of it. I don't know what to do. I can't talk to anyone. I must be a little sick mentally to even consider drinking iodine. I don't want to commit suicide. With my luck, I'd never be born again."

~~~

I ask Mom, "Why'd Dad become a mortician?"

"He wanted to be a doctor but had us to support. It would have taken too long to become a doctor, so he went to mortuary school, a 12-month program. Worsham College of Mortuary Science, near Chicago. He took courses like anatomy, biology, how to rebuild people's faces if they need it, funeral service counseling, the psychology of grief—"

"He took psychology classes?" He needed counseling himself. "Did he regret not becoming a doctor?"

"I don't know."

"Did you ever ask him?"

"Oh, I don't know," she says, defensively, it seems, as though I'm judging or accusing her. "He wanted to be a partner at Kingsley Funeral Home, but Mr. Kingsley offered it to Dan Barrett. I don't know why he chose Dan over your dad who worked there longer."

I'm sorry that Dad didn't get his dream. Something should have worked out for him. "Where'd you and Dad meet?"

"At a USO; a social club for military personnel. And we both worked in a psychiatric ward for soldiers coming back shell-shocked from the war, so we got to know each other better. We helped to administer shock therapy. It was very interesting. A young man came in for a treatment in his pajamas with a Bible in his pocket. He told the supervisor that if we hurt him, God would hurt us in Heaven. I think the session went okay. I worked there a couple years. Your Dad couldn't take it more than a couple weeks and was reassigned to assisting with eye surgeries."

"Why'd you join the WAAC?" I pronounced it "wax." The Women's Auxiliary Army Corps.

"I wanted to see Europe but ended up in California. My biggest regret was majoring in music instead of art in college and then dropping out after two years to join the Army."

So, neither of them had the life they wanted. Well, I expect to achieve my goals and dreams once I figure out what they are.

Mom catches my hand in hers and gives it four quick, playful squeezes. Each squeeze stands for a word: do—you—love—me?

I squeeze back: yes—I—do.

She squeezes: how—much? Now comes the difficult part. I have to squeeze her hand hard enough to let her know that I love her a lot, but not hard enough to crush her bones. But if I don't squeeze really hard, that means there's still some love I'm holding back. So, I rely on body language as well, grasp her hand tightly, grit my teeth, and writhe dramatically to add emphasis to my squeeze.

Only now I realize that in that game, the more you love someone, the more you can hurt her trying to prove it.

8. The Summons

All of us have moments in our childhood where we come alive for the first time. And we go back to those moments and think, this is when I became myself. — Rita Dove

When I was little I wished that I were tall enough to look into the bathroom mirror. I envied how casually Mom and Dad took their height for granted; Mom swirled into the bathroom to check her hair and makeup and swirled out again, Dad shaved and examined his chin in the mirror to be sure that he got it all.

If I could, I'd linger in front of the mirror, look into my eyes. The mirror beckoned me from its height. Something mysterious waited. I dragged a chair over, climbed up on it, and leaned as close as I could to my reflection. I scanned my pupils, looked from one to the other, peered as deeply as I could into them, searching for whatever it was that made me move and breathe and think and look and see. Where had that Something come from and what was it? It moves through me like a resident, looks out the windows of my eyes, listens with my ears, feels with my fingers, tends my thoughts, and orders the beat of my pulse and the rhythm of my breath.

Does everyone have a "Something" in them? I still have mine; people who die don't have theirs anymore—where'd theirs go? It isn't like a hand or a foot. It's steam on a mirror; perfume, a scent I can't smell, a vapor I can't bottle.

Where had the impulse come from—at such an early age—to climb up on a chair and look for Something that lived inside of me? All I saw were my dark pupils, but I knew It was there. It was the impulse behind the desire to look. It was the One doing the looking, the One who animated me and gave me life, the One who summoned me to the mirror.

9. What He Does in There

Embalm: To cheat vegetation by locking up the gases upon which it feeds … many a dead man who ought now to be ornamenting his neighbor's lawn as a tree, or enriching his table as a bunch of radishes, is doomed to a long inutility.
— Ambrose Bierce

I didn't mind living in the apartment over the chapels and the thickly carpeted halls that smelled of pungent flowers; and below the chapels, the embalming room. I wasn't afraid that a body was going to come alive again, stagger zombie-like upstairs, and get me—not after what they went through being embalmed.

They're delivered to the back entrance of the funeral home, taken to the basement, and emerge later, sculpted by my father's artful hands, pink-cheeked in their lustrous, silk-lined coffins.

Dad and I are going to lunch. There's a funeral in the main chapel so I look away as I pass. People's grief embarrasses me because they're so committed to it and self-absorbed.

I wait for Dad in the staff lounge, which has a black-and-white checkered-tile floor and a faded couch. I open the old, white refrigerator stocked with soft drinks, take a root beer, and sit on the couch. The root beer stings the inside of my nose; it needs a scoop of vanilla ice cream to settle the fizz.

No way I'm going into the embalming room; I know what he does in there. He gave a sanitized version to my Girl Scout troop. He did well. He spoke about embalming throughout history—how the Egyptians started it—and how it's now his privilege to prepare the deceased for the funeral so people can honor their loved ones, support each other emotionally, and gain closure. He explained it simply—the worst time in many people's lives—the death of a loved one.

The door opens, and he steps out. He's wearing shorts because it's summer; each of his legs is striped with puffy varicose veins from standing so long every day on the hard floor in the embalming room. "You want to watch?" he asks, hopefully it seems. I shake my head, no, and he disappears back into the embalming room.

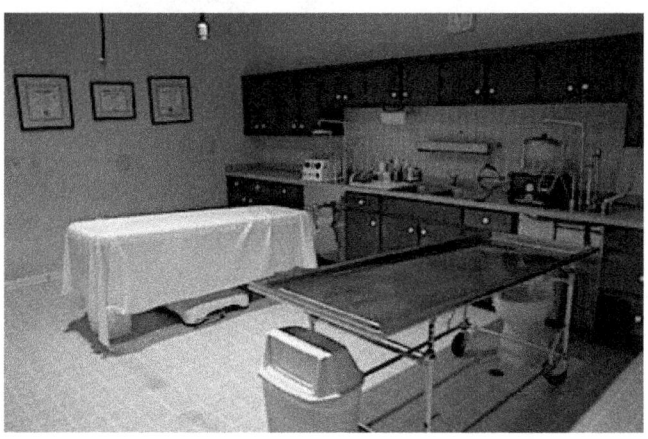

He massages a body to slow rigor mortis and keep the blood from coagulating in the extremities. This keeps the body flexible longer and easier to handle (we call them "bodies" instead of cadavers; seems less ghoulish). He washes the body and covers its private parts with a towel. Then he snips both ends of a vein or artery, attaches the embalming machine to one end, and pumps in the embalming fluid (one-quart fluid per 50 pounds of body weight), which forces the blood to run out and down the stainless-steel gutter on the side of the table into a sink. It'd take a couple quarts of embalming fluid to do me, but I want to be cremated. Dad wants to be cremated, too, which doesn't seem to honor his "art."

Sometime during the procedure, he inserts a long, sharp, metal trocar into various body cavities to release accumulated gas. I don't even want to think where the trocar goes in first, *ewww*. And then, like an upholsterer stuffing a cushion, he packs the mouth, nostrils, and eyes with cotton—or sometimes putty or puts plastic eyecups under the lids—so they retain their shape.

He deals with death daily and dutifully, applying make-up skillfully. And what make-up doesn't accomplish, the lights in the chapel will, the same kind they sometimes use in butcher shops over the counters to make the meat look red and more appetizing.

Aunt Joan (Dad's brother's wife) told me that Dad would drag them in there to show them the latest body he embalmed, and she'd say, "Oh, nice job. I mean, what do you say to something like that?"

I guess we all like some sort of recognition for a job well done.

~~~

Dad likes to surprise people (and our dog HoBeau) in a bad way for his own entertainment. Aunt Pat (Mom's sister) walked up to a body he embalmed and just as she peered into the casket he flicked the lights off and on to scare her. Another time he put a plastic skull in the cleaning woman's basket. She saw it, shrieked, and quit on the spot without giving the customary two-week's notice. And he hoisted Aunt Joan onto the embalming table. She told me, "I never visited him again at work."

Once he sweet talked HoBeau, "Good dog, what a good boy," lulling him into a dreamy state and then leapt at him, *Arrrgh!*" HoBeau went wild, zigzagging all over the den and running in frantic circles. Dad laughed and laughed. He never got another chance to do that. HoBeau was leery of him forever after and avoided him; like I do.

Dad is as short fused as they come and when he yells, the veins on his neck stand out like cables, his face turns red, and his temples throb; if he isn't yelling about something, he's seething, restless and frustrated, or just plain furious with people in general.

My birth certificate claims I'm related to this tormented man, and it must be true—the shape of my face is his, long and oval, my skin has a similar translucence, my eyes are blue like his, I'm tall and I've grown his large, pale hands with long, slender fingers. I'm nervous, too, and we have the same last name.

He seemed bewildered by the responsibility of caring for a little girl who colored with bold colors and sat in the field across the street staring into the weeds talking to herself. I was his ghost child, witch baby, listening to things that weren't there, head cocked slightly so I could hear better.

Everything is covered with a soft fuzz of sound; if I listen with my eyes closed, I can hear the outlines of people in a room and hear the pulse of their thoughts. My hearing's good, the better to hear you with, Mom and Dad. So far, just names and phrases pop into my mind like corks bobbing up from underwater, but I expect to get much better at this. I crave intimacy with the living and aim to listen to them from the insides of their heads, to eavesdrop on their most private thoughts.

Dad watches me as if I'm a riddle he can't solve. He seems to despise the clutter of "inappropriate" behaviors that comprise my childhood and made it clear that he'd tolerate none of it from me, no questions, no idle chatter, no surprises, no noise, nothing. The dead always do what he wants them to, why couldn't I? He dresses them up like dolls and makes them nice. He's amused when relatives lean over the bodies in their caskets and comment, "Oh, he looks just like himself." Dad laughs, "How else do they expect them to look?"

Yes, unlike me, the dead are manageable; he can control them. At first, I resisted his attempts to control me, so he engineered little surprises to catch me off guard. He gained my trust and then startled or tricked me. He was as unpredictable and accurate as a sniper. When I was an infant, he snuck up and set off firecrackers behind me in the living room. Soon after, I was afraid of the candles on my birthday cake, thunder, drums, and flash cameras. Then he ridiculed me for being afraid. If I were dead, could he relate to me better?

"It was awful that he did that with the firecrackers," Mom exclaimed.

~~~

Before I learned to read in kindergarten and could challenge what Dad said, he showed me a picture of a soldier in the newspaper, "He had to have his fingernails pulled out because he got ringworm under them. If you're not careful, you'll get ringworm from the kids at school and have to have your fingernails pulled out."

Be careful, careful, he warned, but didn't tell me what to do to avoid disaster, only that danger, illness, and death are certainties.

~~~

Lissa and I watch *American Bandstand* on TV. My brothers like *Howdy Doody*, which has marionettes with visible strings, and a clown who can't talk so he honks a horn to communicate. Buffalo Bob, an adult, visits with the puppets every day. It's very disturbing.

I watched *Leave it to Beaver* a couple times. Beaver Cleaver is a boring little boy whose parents, June and Ward, never fight. Ward is an accountant and June wears crisp shirtdresses, pearls, and heels to cook and clean. We're nothing like them. Dad's an undertaker and Mom wears Capri pants and rides a bicycle all over town because she doesn't have a driver's license. It's so embarrassing.

My favorite show is *The Twilight Zone* with stories that have chilling endings. There's another strange show, but I don't like it: *The Addam's Family*. They live in an old, castle-like home on North Cemetery Ridge. Morticia, the mom, is beautiful and sullen. Her husband Gomez has bulging eyes. Lurch, the butler, looks like Frankenstein's monster, and all he says is, "You rang?" The kids, Pugsley and Wednesday, are ghouls, and Grandma's a witch. Cousin

Itt came to visit and Gomez got him a job at the zoo, but the zoo staff thought he was an animal and put him on exhibit.

Then there are *The Munsters* who live in a creepy, spider-web-covered house. Herman Munster is a funeral home employee, his wife, Lily, a vampire, 10-year-old son, Edward Wolfgang, a werewolf, and Lily's father, Count Dracula, a mad scientist. They think their niece, Marilyn, is unfortunate because she's young, pretty, and normal. I think I'm the "Marilyn" in my family.

It bothers me that some people think horror is funny or entertaining. They use hearses as personal vehicles just to get from one place to another. Some say it's a comfortable ride or practical—they can haul long pieces of construction material—and others say that they can sleep in the back, like camping, if they cover the casket rollers. I think they do it for the shock value, to draw attention to themselves, or to thumb their noses at death—as if they have any control over it. Who are they trying to fool?

Mom adores *Father Knows Best* on TV about a pleasant family who lives in the Midwest. Jim Anderson is an insurance agent. Every evening he comes home from work, changes out of his suit into comfortable clothes, and deals wisely with his family's problems. Mom marvels at how well they all get along. "Oh sure, they fight sometimes," she says gently, "but they love each other." I just know she's thinking, why can't we be like them.

Mom—slim and pretty, color coordinated, and consistent as dawn—making chicken soup and dumplings and reading me stories when I was little—always there to soften any emotional damage that I sustain in the subtle, unending battle between Dad and me. She must be predictable, or I'll be lost in the tangle of my fears. She must never turn away or I'll go crazy like the man in the insane asylum hitting his head against the bars, the women who tried to run back into the flames, or the children I knew were in there.

The stagnant air in the staff lounge outside the embalming room smells like formaldehyde; I feel queasy. About now he's sealing the body's lips with a thin film of glue that he applies from a small, amber bottle; he showed it to me once and explained what it was for.

He seals the lips shut tight.

Kathleen L. Hawkins

www.DetroitMemories.com

10. The Wigwam

To really ask is to open the door to the whirlwind. The answer may annihilate the question and the questioner. — Anne Rice

Dad emerges from the embalming room, wipes his hands on a towel, "Let's go eat, I'm starved." I follow him into the bright afternoon and slip into the hearse. It's roomy inside and smells like rubber and roses. On our way to lunch Dad pulls over, gets out, and scolds a little boy for playing too close to the road. Dad gestures angrily toward the hearse, the little boy cowers. Welcome to my world, little boy.

Dad gets back in, "I told him that he's going to get himself killed, and when you're dead, you're a long-time dead."

Farther down the road a teenager sees us coming and sticks out his thumb for a ride. "Let's pick him up," I urge. Scare the poo out of him.

"Soon enough," Dad says softly.

~~~

I love The Wigwam cafeteria. There's a huge teepee on the roof, larger-than-life wooden Indians standing by the entrance (it's 1956; the term these days is "Native Americans"), and an interior that's dark like a forest with a woodsy motif. A waterfall splashes 10-feet down the mossy rocks on one wall into a fishpond strewn with shiny pennies and stocked with large, fantail goldfish. I stand as close as I can to the waterfall to catch the mist on my face.

The restaurant smells like roast turkey and coffee. I slide a heavy tray along a gleaming counter, and select deep-dish chicken pie with a flakey crust, a green salad with bleu cheese dressing, and a piece of hot apple pie with cinnamon sauce. Then I choose a table in the corner next to a picture of two Indian braves on their horses beside a lovely stream. Diffused light behind the picture lends a realistic quality to it. A thick slab of glass on the table covers an arrangement of sphagnum moss, leaves, and a large iridescent, swallowtail butterfly with paper-thin wings.

www.DetroitMemories.com

"Bring me a pitcher of water and leave it on the table," Dad tells the server. "I drink a lot of water. I'm an embalmer, I get dehydrated from the formaldehyde I use."

I'm mortified. The server looks at him blankly and complies.

We eat in silence, and I then tell Dad, "I got an 'A' in band and journalism on my report card."

"Those are worthless subjects."

"And my essay 'The Onion Field' won honorable mention in the Scholastic Writing Awards contest. It's about when I topped onions on Harrison's farm."

"*Ah huh.*" He holds his water glass up to the light; he squints to determine what's floating in it, a lemon seed or something else, like dirt. Or maybe there was a fingerprint on the glass.

I persist, "The essay was about how topping onions was an adventure for me, but for the migrant workers, that's their lives."

"*Um.*"

"Now I'm writing a story called 'Journey to the Center of the System' about some people who shrink themselves and go on a journey to the center of a human body where they have all kinds of adventures. It's tricky in the lungs because that's like being caught in a tornado and they get blown around and separated from each other."

He rolls a handful of pens across the table to me. I see the imprint: "Frigid Fluid." He's a part-time sales rep for the Frigid Fluid Company, which sells products to the funeral industry: cemetery equipment, embalming fluid, and urns.

I continue, "And the people in my story almost drown in the kidneys, in the urine."

"What good does it do you to write stories? You write them and then just put them away."

"It gives me something to do, and I enjoy looking back and reading them again. What do you see in embalming bodies?"

"Don't knock it. It keeps food on the table. Do you want your pie warmed? How about more cinnamon sauce? You're all out."

"It's fine, thanks, and I don't need any more sauce."

He seems eager to do something for me as if he realizes that lunch is almost over, and he has yet to please me. He flags down the server, "Bring her more cinnamon sauce and be sure it's warm." He sighs deeply, "I wish your mother would quit that job of hers."

"You wanted her to get a job to help pay the bills."

"I didn't want her to work nights, not at a convalescent home."

"That was the only job that would let her be home with us during the day."

"She's going to get sick, have a heart attack, and die, and when she does, remember that I told you she would. I told her, too. I told her that she'd *die*."

"She just interviewed for a day job in a doctor's office. Nights were hard on her. She seems tired a lot of the time."

"If she gets that office job, she'll have to start right away *and* give them two weeks' notice at the nursing home. She'll have to work day *and* night, which will *kill* her."

He hands me some money. "Buy something feminine to wear. I worry about your mother's influence. She dresses like a man."

My stomach tightens. "That's the tailored look," I say apprehensively.

"I don't like it," he says darkly, and then more menacingly, "Her friends are horsy, if you know what I mean."

What's he implying? Mom has a couple friends, Lissa's mom, who isn't 'horsy,' and Mrs. Hegel, my sixth-grade teacher. Mrs. Hegel is also the girls' gym teacher. She has short hair, wears slacks, and kind of walks like a man. Of all the teachers I've had so far, she's not one of my favorites for some reason.

Whenever Mrs. Hegel comes to visit Mom, I have to clean my room, dust, and vacuum. I resent her visits, although I don't know why; is it because of the extra cleaning that Mom makes me do or because Mrs. Hegel might judge my hairstyle? Mom thinks my hair is a mess, a terrible sight. Unlike hers, which is naturally wavy, mine is straight and fine. I like to wear it long and pulled back in a ponytail; it's so easy that way, but Mom insists that it should be short and fluffy and frame my face like her and Mrs. Hegel's hair frames their faces. Mom sets my hair in curlers every night. She gets a glass of warm water, a comb, and prickly curlers, and turns on the TV so I have something to watch instead of gripe about having my hair set. And then I sleep on the uncomfortable curlers.

Mom and Mrs. Hegel are friends at church, too. Mom can't stand to miss one Sunday.

Dad speaks slowly, his voice low, "I think we better watch your mother."

I run my fingertips over the tabletop and trace the outline of a splendid butterfly under the glass. It lived a few short weeks and now here it is, pressed forever on display in a dimly lit restaurant called The Wigwam.

"I have to go," Dad says and puts his napkin on the table. "I have another body waiting; you know how it is."

I trudge after him. He's good at what he does. I'm confident that nothing will come alive again when he's done with it—including Mom and me.

11. Unattached Clusters, Improper Shutdown

Swear to make them cut me open, so I won't be buried alive.
— Frederic Chopin's last words

Early computer users sometimes saw the following message when they turned off their computers: "Unattached clusters, improper shutdown."

How did unattached clusters come to be: operator error, computer error, or random occurrence? And where'd they go when the computer was shut down improperly; were they out floating around in cyberspace? If people knew what caused them, could they prevent them in some way, maybe by "defragging" the hard drive or simply deleting the unattached clusters and they'd go away?

~~~

Dad does carpentry to make extra money. He builds cupolas, bookshelves, and fancy window frames—and then surprised us by building an addition—complete with a fireplace—onto our house. We use it as a family room where we put the nice table when company comes. The rest of the time we eat at the kitchen table, which now doubles as a confessional. Dad and I are sitting at it; Mom and the boys are somewhere else. Dad seems ready to say something, either trying to figure out how to say it or to summon the courage. I suppose it's another ghastly story.

The clock ticks. I wait for him to speak. Tiny specks of dust float in a sunbeam streaming through the window. Then he tells me.

I didn't think about his confession for years, but it must have been rattling around in my psyche, an unattached cluster that I couldn't delete.

It wasn't murder. There was no intent to kill the man; Dad thought he was dead. Everyone agreed that he was dead; the doctors "called" the time of death and someone called Dad.

There's no name for what Dad did, no precedent. There are things in life that happen for which there are no names. But had this secret come out, it might have cost him his job.

I didn't know what to think. Why did he tell *me*? I'm a kid. I can't do anything about it. Maybe he can't confide in other embalmers; it might make him look bad or ruin his reputation. And he and Mom rarely talk to each other anymore except to argue.

Years later a friend says, "Maybe he just needed to tell someone, so he told you; you could have just been a fence post."

Those were the choices? Either he told me grown-up things I wasn't meant to hear, confided in me things I couldn't do anything about, made me responsible for his absolution—or I could have been a fence post?

Decades later, in the safety of my own home, I peer down through the years into the dark tunnel of his confession and ask, "Didn't you know the man was still alive?"

"I thought he was dead. I had a death certificate."

"But you said that you had a strange feeling."

"Yes, like he was watching me."

"Then why didn't you stop embalming him?"

"I was doing my job."

I'm reminded of pilots doing their jobs on a final descent in a storm, should they take a chance and land or fly safely to the next airport? How many have thought, "*Aw*, hell, we're so close to home, I don't want a bunch of pissed off passengers, let's just go for it, it'll be fine." How many ignore their gut instinct and how many people die because of it?

I couldn't make sense of Dad's admission, relate to it, or attach it to anything I ever heard or read about—and I wasn't able to offer him redemption like a priest or a minister might. I didn't know how to feel about it. But a confession like Dad's burrows deep into the psyche and takes root. It forever changed the way I thought about life, death, and consciousness.

I was 15, and I thought there were only two extremes: life and death, black and white, all or nothing, but that day I learned that there are degrees of consciousness—and I've have spent my whole life since then trying to understand them and live as fully as possible.

Dad and I rarely talk about anything significant, and then when he does, I'm silent.

"Tonight, while I was working on a body, I had the feeling that he wasn't quite dead. Like he was watching me while I worked."

What am I supposed to do with that? Psychologists tell people not to burden children with adult issues, like what the parents fight about, or expect a boy to be the man of the house if his dad runs off, or tell your daughter that you might have killed a man by embalming him.

In those days, there were two criteria for being dead: breathing stops, the heart stops, and boom, you're dead. Today we know that the body shuts down in stages: heart, breath, pupils, and brain. At any one of those stages it could be possible to call the person back into the body and save the life that's slipping away.

Who was the man: in his 20s, 40s, or older, someone's father, husband, uncle, brother? Was a grieving family making funeral arrangements while my dad did his work?

I've heard about people who hover over operating tables during their own surgeries and, afterwards, repeat things that the doctors said and did—or, even creepier, regain consciousness in the morgue.

Dad spent the next few days in a far away, contemplative mood sitting in his big leather chair in the living room. He seemed disturbed to a depth I'd never seen before. His eyes regained their focus eventually and he never spoke of that day again.

We want a life that continues forever, that never runs down or runs out, that resists entropy and defies physical laws. We seek magic and beauty in something eternal. We're hybrids who exist on a physical and a spiritual plane at the same time, or maybe there is no duality, maybe the material world is spiritual through and through to the core. And yet, imagine watching from a distance while the undertaker does his work: your internal organs and cavities pierced slowly one at a time with a trocar, your blood drained and replaced with "Frigid Fluid," eyes and lips glued shut, and you know that you can never come back, but oh, for a moment, there'd been a chance.

~~~

Dad's confession is so incomprehensible that I wonder if I'll ever understand how it affected me. I tell a friend, "This was the hardest chapter of all to write in the whole book."

"Because it was so emotional?" he asks gently.

"No, because it wasn't."

12. Cumberland Gap

There is always one moment in childhood when the door opens and lets the future in. — Graham Greene

My brother Matt is concerned that I'll leave out the good times in my story and he emails me some memories that he has of spending time with Dad:

> We ate lunch out together, Dad came to the campus grill to have a burger when I was a short order cook, and he came in for steak and eggs and to "flirt" with the waitresses; they competed to wait on him. He didn't come for the "excellent" short order steaks; he came to see me! He took me and my friend who didn't have a father to see the Harlem Globe Trotters and Red Wings Hockey. We shot the .38 together. He impersonated President Nixon over dinner at Sindbad's Seafood Restaurant and we boated on the Detroit River with sodas and swam along the Canadian shoreline. Dad taught me to drive (Buick Skylark), buttoned my tuxedo shirt on prom night, etc.

A friend encourages me to "Leave out the good memories; they weaken the story. Keep it strong and horrible like in the book about child abuse, *A Child Called It*."

But it's because of the good times that the bad times were more glaring. I never knew when emotional chaos was going to break into a perfectly fine day, like criminals break into a house to steal valuables. I was tense, guarded, always on alert. I had anxiety like a low-grade fever just below the threshold of consciousness; but the anxiety was there, nevertheless, affecting my sense of safety and my joy.

Mom and Dad were loving, kind, and supportive—until they weren't. The exceptions came out as rage and ridicule (Dad), and a severe whipping once when Mom thought that Bill and I were about to fight over a banana peel he pushed in front of me on the table. I pushed it back, "I don't want your banana peel."

She got Dad's heavy, black belt and beat us into the corners of the room, crying "I can't stand it, I can't take it anymore!"

I was glad she was whipping two of us so maybe she'd get tired faster and stop sooner. Later while I was crying in my room, she came in and apologized. I saw her whip Bill severely another time when he was a little boy headed toward the busy street in front of our house. She wanted to teach him to never go near the street.

When I was eight, I vowed to be so good that I'd never be "spanked" again. Mom said that Grandfather told her, speaking of me, "Kathleen's smart. Don't be too strict with her."

Matt posted on Facebook, "We kids had a good home with a mother and father both present who supplied us a 'steady' home, security, food, heat and utilities. No drinking and no beatings. Mom met her two granddaughters multiple times … Time with them in the kitchen cooking and many group hugs."

Bill emailed me a news story about a man who killed his mother with a claw hammer. He exclaimed, "See, we didn't have it so bad." Of course, other kids had it "worse," comparatively (like the boy in *A Child Called It*), but to dwell on *his* misery would be to minimize my feelings, dismiss them, and feel guilty for feeling the way I did. It'd be brushing my feelings aside, an "easy" way out so I won't have to face it, think about it, or do anything about it ever again. That's a way to repress legitimate feelings. Writer that I am, analytic soul, I want to understand something the best I can before I let it go.

Spiritual philosophies say to focus on the positive, forgive the negative; I believe that, too, but I don't want to do it too soon. Some people also say that our experiences—even horrifying, heart-wrenching circumstances, like being sexually assaulted, losing someone we love to a natural disaster, or being ridiculed as a child—were for our personal or spiritual growth. Sure, maybe people can gain wisdom or understanding eventually, but if I feel that awful experiences are for my personal growth, I worry that I might have attracted the disaster somehow or I feel guilty for not just getting over it or for withdrawing to protect myself, for going silent, for not being able to fix a toxic situation. My self-esteem tanks.

I could try to gloss over my feelings, but the body remembers. I flinch if someone raises a hand to reach for something, my skin crawls if someone stands too close behind me, I startle easily, I avoid social situations, and I hate to be watched. Even though Mom and Dad were kind and supportive much of the time, exceptions set the pace. Because there could be sudden "explosions"—with anger or the belt—on the most ordinary of days, I began to fear the calm.

~~~

I was born three years before Bill, and seven before Matt. We each entered the family at different times in my parents' marriage. I was there for the beginning and the unraveling, Bill, for the unraveling, and Matt, for the unraveling and the end. I was off to college (Eastern Michigan University and then San Francisco State), Bill was off to Vietnam (he enlisted), and Matt was still in high school. Quite naturally, we have different perspectives. Our individual lives were affected by nature, nurture, the time in history, education, friends, personal experiences, skills and talents, current culture (books, movies, music), personal choices, and decisions.

Yes, there were good times. Dad taught me to ride a two-wheel bicycle; I remember the moment I found the right balance and pedaled off and away from him and he grew smaller in the distance. And I remember he took me to the Wigwam for lunches, to

Sindbad's restaurant for dinner on the Detroit River where he kept his cabin cruiser, and to Howard Johnson's for their fried-clam platter. And when I got a job as a waitress at a Big Boy restaurant, he came in frequently, ordered pie and coffee, was pleasant, and left me a five-dollar tip. I liked having him come in.

    Mom took us places, too, like the Detroit Zoo. I especially liked the polar bears splashing in the icy water of their large exhibit. And she took us to Canada's Bob-Lo Island, an amusement park in the middle of the Detroit River. It was an 18-mile ride on one of two large steamships, the Columbia or the St. Claire (passenger capacity 2,566, and 2,416, respectively). There were also family trips to visit cousins in Iowa and grandparents in Wisconsin.

    I remember the lakes: Cass and Kensington where we went to boat, swim, and picnic, and Black Lake where we vacationed in a rented cabin on the beach. There were trips to Yates Cider Mill every autumn. I loved the cold, tart cider, the soft, warm donuts, being in the country, and the vibrant fall colors.

    And I remember our birthday present to Jesus each Christmas: a beautifully wrapped box with a narrow opening in the top, which we put on the fireplace mantle. Mom put a pad of paper and a pencil next to it. Whenever we did something good, we wrote it down and put it in the box.

I was tempted to peek in the box and read the good deeds that Mom, Dad, and the boys did, but I didn't. As much as I love to know people's secrets—maybe that's the writer in me—I respect boundaries and don't snoop.

On Christmas Eve we put the box, unopened, in the fireplace and watched it burn. One year I cut up "color cakes," round, wax cakes containing certain chemicals that turn flames various colors. People set them on top of logs in a fireplace or a campfire. So, I cut them up and pushed them into the slot in the top of our Christmas box. I wanted Mom and Dad to marvel at the beautiful colors and believe that Jesus was pleased with our good deeds.

And, maybe, part of *me* wanted to feel that *I* contributed something lovely and of value to the season and to our family. They watched the flames a while, and Mom commented, "It must be something in the wrapping paper that's turning the flames colors."

The tree was beautifully lit and covered with tinsel (hung a strand at a time, as Mom taught us, rather than tossed haphazardly in bunches onto the tree). We sang carols and hymns. Mom said, "Remember this when you're grown up." The cozy den, the fireplace, the tree, the singing, and the dog lying on the braided rug by the hearth; so peaceful, the night before Christ's birthday.

~~~

My favorite piece of music to play in the high school band is "Cumberland Gap" (there's a bluegrass song by the same name, but *my* "Cumberland Gap" was the first). Mom and Dad come early to my concerts to get a front row seat. Dad leaves his pager in the car. He stopped going to church because his pager might go off during the service; a convenient excuse because he didn't like church? My concerts are different. They're the only time the dead must wait.

We practiced during the year and are ready for the concert. I snap open my clarinet case, unscrew the lid on the small, round container of cork grease—smell the odd, pleasant scent—take the lovely wooden clarinet, piece by piece, out of the case, apply cork grease where needed, and assemble it. I scoop up the sheet music, take my seat on stage behind the curtains with the others, and suck on the reed to make it pliable before securing it to the mouthpiece.

I'm second-chair clarinet out of 27. As a freshman, I was thrilled when I aced the try-outs and got to sit in the first row with the senior boys. First chair clarinets play the melody, which is great for me because I have trouble harmonizing.

The curtain opens. The concert begins. We alternate selections—fast and lively, slow and grand—and then it's time for "Cumberland Gap." We proceed deliberately, much like hikers working their way up to the top of "Tri-State Peak," the point where Virginia, Kentucky, and Tennessee all come together; when we get there, the other instruments fall silent, and the wind instruments take over, the earth drops out from underneath me and I soar out over the valley. I live for that exhilarating moment, breaking free, Mom and Dad in the front row watching. Do they know that I'm flying?

Cumberland Gap on a Foggy Morning
https://commons.wikimedia.org/w/index.php?curid=898801

13. Caravans of Silence
Silence is a text easy to misread. — A.A. Attanasio

My brothers squirm and punch each other next to me in the back seat of the car and keep bumping into me. I hate family vacations. What other 16-year old endures such agony? They stop wrestling and exclaim frantically, "Hold your breath, hold your breath."

There's a cemetery ahead. We have to hold our breath when we pass one, so we don't inhale any departed spirits floating around looking for live bodies to inhabit (never mind that I lived above funeral homes when I was little and probably inhaled everybody's spirit before we moved into our new house). It's probably a myth about holding your breath, but I'm going to do it just in case, but not until the last second. This cemetery is next to the longest traffic light in town.

There are three cars in this pitiful caravan; ours is last with me and the boys in the back seat, Mom is driving (she got a driver's license finally), and her new friend Janine is sitting next to her. In the car ahead of us are Dad and his friend Janine who does make-up in one of the funeral homes (can you believe it, each of them has a Janine). Mom met her Janine (whose hair is short and fluffy and frames her face) at the lake (I don't know where I was on that day). In the lead car, we've got Mom's Janine's husband and their kids.

The cars are packed with camping gear, tents and Coleman grills, coolers, picnic baskets, and swimming suits. I'd just die if anyone at school knew that I was on a family vacation—and with *two* Janines. The cemetery looms ahead.

Dad and his Janine go on "business" trips, but don't talk about it. Where do they go, anyway, to casket conventions? Shopping for hearses? I'm sure they're having an affair. How can she be interested in him? He's uptense (uptight + tense; sometimes I make up words).

Aw, crud, the light turned red; the first two cars in our caravan zip through, but ever the good driver, Mom brakes. The cars ahead pull off the side of the road to wait for us. My brothers and I take deep breaths and settle in for a long light next to the gravestones.

It's quiet in the car, which gives me time to mull over Dad's allegations about Mom and her Janine being "involved."

I think Dad's delusional and should be institutionalized. In fact, Uncle Don (Dad's brother) told me that Dad was hospitalized with a nervous condition for three months when he was 14 (Dad never mentioned it). Uncle Don said it was St. Vitus Dance, when a person can't stop shaking and jerking. Apparently, it's a physical condition, but their mother told Dad that he got sick because he must have touched himself "down there."

Well, Dad's mistaken about what he says regarding Mom. She and Janine are just friends; that's all, period. Mom is a typical mom—baking pie and waiting for me to come home from school and tell her about my day. She must be predictable, or I'd be lost like in that game where they blindfold you and turn you around to disorient you and then watch you try to find your way: "turn around once and you're lost." If Mom likes women as Dad implies, a judge might award custody of me to Dad and then I'd die, I'd just die.

It's getting harder to hold my breath. The gravestones beside the car can wait forever; I can't. I feel faint and there's a burning sensation in my chest. The world is going gray; I'm going to pass out. I lean forward to divert my attention from my lungs and peer into the front seat. Mom and Janine are holding hands on the seat between them. In the rearview mirror, Mom's eyes are shining with a new and different light. I gasp and start to breathe again, greedy for air—gulping—inhaling spirit after spirit after spirit.

The Mortician's Child

I think that I became invisible gradually in my family, rather than all at once because of a single event. Mom and Dad are preoccupied with their respective jobs and their Janines. I keep a low profile; they don't seem to notice me anymore.

I'm running down the sand hill at the lake, arms spinning like a windmill as I try to keep my balance. Halfway down there's a tree stump and I step up on it. There are boats in the distance, a smell of charcoal, barbecues, and suntan lotion with coconut oil, the sound of kids playing. I jump off the stump onto the angle of sand, my right leg twists underneath me, and I land on it with my full weight.

It feels really odd. It aches deep inside, like it'd throw up if legs could throw up. I take a few steps, it gives out; I collapse in the sand. I limp to the parking lot and lean against the car.

Mom and Dad are carrying the grill, sandy beach towels, wet swimming suits, video camera, suntan lotion, deflated air mattress, beach blankets, and the cooler. Mom is trying to round up the boys. I stand by the car. As far as I can see, everything is moving—except me. I broke my leg, and no one noticed.

It's summer so I don't have to go to school and get to sit around. I can walk a few steps before my leg gives out, so I stay within reach of chairs, tables, and the couch to break a possible fall.

Mom and Dad don't see that I'm having trouble walking, and I don't tell them that something's wrong. I bought into the "be strong" family ethic so thoroughly that it hardly occurs to me that my leg might be broken. The bone isn't sticking out of the skin, like a compound fracture, and there's no bump, so I make do, like an injured animal gives the appearance of strength so its enemies don't peck it to death.

But I can't ignore the pain. I finally tell Dad, as nonchalantly as I can, "My leg hurts ever since I fell on it at the lake."

He looks it up and down, "It doesn't look broken."

"Okay," I relent, with some hesitation. And I spend the next month favoring it. Lissa comes to my house instead of me going to hers, and when we go to the lake, I don't run around, I simply float in the lifebelt, and watch everyone else. It's a month, at least, before I can walk again easily.

~~~

Years later, as an adult, I have problems with my right knee: it's painful, swollen, and keeps locking up. A doctor examines the x-rays, "Your broken leg healed nicely." He points to a white line across the large bone below the knee on my right leg.

There it is: medical proof. I broke my leg when I was 16, and walked on it until it healed "nicely," the broken place unnoticed until someone had a reason and the means to look deeply enough to see it.

As for my sore knee, nothing wrong there. I studied it and noticed that I twisted it when I turned instead of turning on the ball of my foot. A slight adjustment in the way I walked, and all better.

Thinking back on those days, I realize that when I was growing up, there were layers upon layers of silences—fog, curtains, and mist, vaporous and vague—so many questions caught in the pleats of the silences, which magnify our internal chatter. It's easy to interpret someone's silence with our own fears and to expect the worst: waiting for the phone to ring when someone's overdue, being on the receiving end of the punitive "silent treatment," waiting patiently or desperately for a parent's explanation or a spouse's apology.

Silences keep us from knowing the truth and lock us out of each other's lives with no chance for understanding, forgiveness, or redemption. In silences, there's no closure or clarity. How easily and thoughtlessly we squander our time with each other.

14. Variations on a Theme

There is strength in the differences between us ...
comfort where we overlap. — Ani Difranco

When I was a baby, I was afraid to be left in the church nursery while Mom attended the adult service—and I expressed my fear loudly—so she took me with her into the sanctuary. I snuggled in her lap throughout the first part of the service, and then got restless, so she opened her purse, pulled out a familiar white linen handkerchief filled with Cheerios, and I settled down again, munching happily on the dry cereal, and was quiet the rest of the service.

I'm older now and I pray as instructed in Sunday school: "Our Father who art in Heaven, hallowed be thy name, lead us not into temptation, but deliver us from evil."

Mom says, "Here's how I like to say it: Our Father who art in Heaven, hallowed be thy name, *leave* us not in temptation, but deliver us from evil."

And I sing: "Amazing Grace how sweet the sound that saved a wretch like me."

Mom says: "Let's say this instead, how sweet the sound that saved a *soul* like me."

And at Halloween I go door to door calling: "Trick or treat!"

Mom tells me: "Say 'Help the poor' instead." She didn't like the implication that we'd retaliate against someone who didn't give us a treat. I tried "help the poor," but didn't feel poor so I called out "Happy Halloween," instead, and that felt just right.

The minister speaks about "predestination" and how God determines in advance who's going to heaven and who's going to hell and sends them there regardless of how good or bad they've been. "That's not fair," I tell Mom. "What's the point of living a good life if God just plans to send you to hell? Is there a quota for how many people get into heaven? Can it only hold so many?"

She puts her usual positive spin things, "I prefer to think that 'predestination' means that God knows ahead of time the choices we're going to make—heaven or hell—he doesn't send us there." Then she adds softly, "I believe that heaven and hell are states of mind rather than actual places."

I comment, "Then everyone should go to Heaven if they live a good life. We should be there right now while we're still alive."

And the Ten Commandments? "Those are *predictions*," she says, "you *shall not* do those things, like steal, murder, and so on, once you're spiritually mature and aware."

She continues to turn me gently toward the idea that God is consistently loving rather than a vengeful God of storms and lighting bolts, which he uses to kill or hurt people when he's angry.

At first it feels subversive to change lyrics, hymns, and prayers but it makes sense to me, ultimately, to choose the more life-affirming variations. And because she doesn't stick exactly to the accepted rule of "law," to the way things are done and said, it makes sense that she'd create her own variation of love.

~~~

I venture into Christian Science by way of Mary Baker Eddy's book, *Science and Health*. She believed that illness had a spiritual cause and, therefore, needed to be cured spiritually. She felt that we don't need doctors to cure illness. In her book, she says: "All is infinite Mind and its infinite manifestation, for God is All-in-All."

I feel a pleasant tingling in my solar plexus when I read that "All is infinite Mind," which feels incredibly right and true to me, and then I read: "Spirit is immortal Truth; matter is mortal error." *Uh oh*, "error" turns me off, perfectionist that I am. If God is "All in All," then God is matter, too, right? But Christian Scientists—or some of them—perceive illness as a failure of faith. When I broke my leg it seemed real enough; was it only error thought, my imagination? Maybe certain emotions, like despair, could also be considered failures of faith, like not trusting that things will turn out for the best. *Science and Health* has small print and ideas I don't understand so I put it respectfully back on the shelf.

~~~

Mom stands by the living room window looking into the sunset, her lips moving silently in what I imagine is prayer, and later I hear her sobbing in their bedroom while Dad's at work. She's desperately unhappy. I'm so afraid that she'll kill herself without warning and one day won't be here, like that young man Dad told me about who committed suicide in his garage. I don't know how to help Mom or what I'd do if she left. I feel helpless and immobilized with fear.

~~~

They put me in advanced, eighth-grade English, which thrills me because I don't have to study grammar. I don't know a gerund from an intransitive verb, and I don't care. Instead of making us learn the parts of speech, the teacher has us read Ralph Waldo Emerson, Henry David Thoreau, and other "transcendentalists" who write about rising above circumstances and perceiving an ultimate, glorious Reality behind all things. They write about a spiritual state that transcends the physical and can be realized by intuition rather than religious doctrine.

What does "ultimate Reality" look like and how do I get there? I'm desperate to transcend Dad's horror stories and rages, Mom's depressions, the two of them fighting, and my social awkwardness. I want to move through life gracefully and wise. I enjoy the sermons on Sundays, but nothing has helped so far, not church, not Bible stories or Bible classes, not Youth Group on Sundays. Nothing!

My first emotion, minutes after I was born, was frustration. People tell me that I can't remember that far back, but I do, I remember the feeling. Sometimes doctors hold newborns up by the ankles and smack them on the bottom to get them to cry so their lungs fill with air. I remember dangling in the air, someone holding me firmly by the ankles, and me trying to swim away from what was holding me back. I didn't see who was holding me; my eyes were either closed or unfocused. Mom said I cried; no slap was necessary.

~~~

I'm 15 years old, sitting in the sanctuary of Westminster Presbyterian Church in Detroit, a tenor is singing a stirring solo. I feel cool—oddly so—my breathing slows, and a great stillness comes over me, moves through me. My senses shut down, fall away, I hover somewhere else, suspended in another form in another dimension in a radiant realm, joined with the splendid Spirit that summoned me to the mirror when I was a child, and it claims me with its fierce, exquisite power. Every cell of my body, brain, mind, and heart hums to the core—no, *from* the core like a great generator.

Photo by Kristen G. https://www.yelp.com/biz_photos/westminster-church-of-detroit-detroit?select=sBZHBp0ZGRkFex4FCXuKDA

Years later Mom validates my fears about her wanting to commit suicide: "The only reason I didn't kill myself was because I had three little children who depended on me."

Growing up I sensed that she wanted out, that she was just one step away from the blade, the cliff, or the highway overpass; I lived with that fear.

And, as a teenager, I lived with another unsettling concern. Dad intercepted me in the narrow hallway, put his finger down the front of my swimming suit—in my cleavage—and flicked his finger back and forth against my breasts.

Aghast, I pulled away.

He shouted, "As long as you live in this house, you'll do what I say!" Then he blinked as if he just realized how inappropriate that was for him to have said.

I was left with a horrifying thought. Did he think of me in a sexual way? Was it simply a passing fantasy for him or something on which he dwelled?

~~~

I came home from college one weekend and found him despondent. "Your mother left me. She moved to Flint to be closer to Janine."

Mom stayed for us, her children—one of us now in college, one in the Marines, and one in high school. Bill and I were grown, and Matt nearly so. And now she had to be on her way.

So, love is why she stayed. And love is why she left.

15. Hammerhead Stall

And the day came when the risk to remain tight in the bud was more painful than the risk to blossom. — Anais Nin

> Aerobatic maneuvers are flight paths
> that put planes in abrupt changes and
> unusual "attitudes" (orientation and
> position in relation to the horizon) in
> air shows and competitions

I'm 18, in my first year of college at Eastern Michigan University. I'm staying in Jones Residence Hall, on campus, and I have a roommate.

Some of the girls are reading *The Feminine Mystique*, about "the problem that has no name." The author Betty Friedan maintains that many women these days aren't happy just being married and having children because they've lost their personal identities. The "feminine mystique" is the mistaken notion that women are naturally fulfilled by devoting their lives to being housewives and mothers.

Sigmund Freud saw women as childlike and destined to be housewives, their roles to be: "In youth an adored darling and in mature years a loved wife." He thought that women who wanted careers were neurotic and might upset the social balance. Yuck! I assumed that I'd go to college and have a career; there was never any question about it.

I like living in the dorm, but my roommate wants to move to an apartment with a couple other women, upperclassmen. I didn't want to be left out, so when they invited me along, I became the fourth woman in an apartment at the College Town Apartments; one of two apartments of women in the 86-apartment complex.

Away from home for the first time and surrounded by guys! But Dad's warnings still ring in my ears, "Boys only want one thing from you and once they get it, they're gone. Why buy the cow when they can get the milk for free?"

> Aerobatics consist of five basic maneuvers:
> lines (horizontal and vertical), loops, rolls,
> spins, and hammerheads

Okay, from everything I've read and been told, nice girls don't have sex before marriage, get rich, like math, ask for anything, get angry, drink, win awards, let boys know that they (the girls) are smart, burp, fart, spit, or sweat, make it to the top, negotiate, lead, beat men at sports, swear, take seconds, kiss on the first date, brag, nag, shout, or fight, scratch themselves in public, wear white shoes after Labor Day, flirt, call boys first, kiss other girls, talk about money, order expensive menu items, speak up, sail boats, drive buses or taxis, pilot airplanes, date two men at a time, go all the way, enjoy sex, touch themselves "down there" below the belt, or touch someone else "down there."

Good grief. Except for piloting a plane, driving a bus or taxi, beating a man at sports (I'm not athletic), or kissing a girl, I expect to do everything on the list more than once. I'm still reserved, quietly independent and stubborn, but away from home at last and ready to test the boundaries.

At first, I was afraid that I might not like men, given that Dad is a bad role model, and Mom maybe doesn't like men in *that* way, at all. I was in the sixth grade when I felt horny for the first time. Blame Elvis Presley, the popular rock-and-roll singer on TV who rotated his hips suggestively, and his voice was so deliberately seductive!

Now, in college, I can't walk, talk, breathe, or wake up in the morning without feeling turned on. They say that men think about sex every 10 seconds. I have them beat by five—on a bad day; on a good day, I think about it every second. And if I'm not consciously thinking about it, there's an undercurrent like a fever throbbing, humming, I can't stand clothes against my body—the fabric, sway, and the cut of them turn me on, but if I take them off, that's worse.

> A "loop" is when a pilot pulls the plane up vertically, continues around until it's heading back in the same direction, making a 360-degree turn like making a loop in a ribbon

So how is it that I'm so lucky to have you? We met at a dance, my first year of college, your senior year; you're studying to be a junior-high school teacher. Clean cut and pleasant. Tall, slim, nice looking and, best of all, loving, thoughtful, and affectionate; you don't yell like Dad. And, surprise, you're from Flint, where Mom moved.

You take me to dinner, movies, parties, and dances. The Beatles are all the rage: "I Want to Hold Your Hand," "Love Me Do," and "Do You Want to Know a Secret," but I like Roy Orbison better, "Pretty Woman," "In Dreams," and "Only the Lonely." "Today" by the New Christy Minstrels is suggestive and romantic: "I'll feast at your table, I'll drink your sweet wine." Then there's "Come a Little Bit Closer" by Jay and the Americans. Barbara Streisand's "People" (people who need people are the luckiest people in the world) confounds me. I'm not convinced that it's "lucky" to need people.

The "Twist" is popular and "The Stroll." I like fast dances and line dances where we don't touch. I have trouble slow dancing; the man is supposed to lead and, as hard as I try, I just can't follow.

I've never been loved. I've felt shy and unattractive most of my life. Mom says, "You could be so pretty if you'd just do something with your hair and wear a little make-up."

I'm pretty enough for Dad.

I go home with you to meet your parents. After dinner we're visiting over dessert and your mother announces, "Your father is suing me for a divorce for having an affair, of which I'm guilty." She seems defiant rather than remorseful; your dad, defeated rather than angry.

You and I clean up in silence after dinner, wash and dry the dishes, put them away. You look at me with pain in your eyes, and maybe embarrassment; I return the look with sympathy. We never speak of it again.

I don't ask what you're feeling. I have trouble talking about emotions. Would it help you if I said my mom's having an affair, too, but with a woman, and Dad's having an affair (they're both named Janine). And remember, when you came to my house for dinner, Dad told you, "I suppose this isn't right, but my daughter turns me on."

I was horrified. I felt sick to my stomach. I hope you didn't think that I was involved with my father in *that* way. What did Dad hope to communicate to you? That you and he had something in common? You didn't respond, and we never discussed it. I didn't know what to say about anything in my life. Instead, I write. I write.

~~~

You and I make out—a lot—but I don't know how to get *there* from here, from making out to "going all the way" and having sex.

In high school I went roller skating (there was a skating rink in town) with a guy from school who was more a friend than anything else. Other guys in school flirted with me, and I certainly liked them: the senior guys in the first clarinet section in band, boys in my classes, boys at church, boys stocking shelves at the grocery store. Lissa was right; I was boy crazy, but I felt bewildered, awkward, and getting lonelier by the second. Deena and another girl at school, Doris, were talking about the dates they had for the weekend. Deena

The Mortician's Child

was going on a hayride, and Doris, to a movie. Deena turned to me and said in a condescending tone, "What are you going to do this weekend, babysit?"

What a snide thing to say. I wanted to punch her. I didn't even have a babysitting job.

My only real "date" in high school was when I was 17. Chuck, the captain of a rival track team, asked me out. We met at a band concert, went out twice, and he kissed me—my first kiss. Monumental! His lips were soft and interesting. Here's what I wrote in my journal:

> Chuck gave me a great gift—my first kiss and my sanity (of course I don't believe that everyone, or anyone for that matter, is entirely sane, but he has helped me). Maybe now I won't be so involved in a world that isn't real.

That first kiss made me feel real. That was the last time he asked me out.

> A roll is rotating the plane using the hinged-wing flaps, and can be done in increments of 360 degrees, such as four, short 90-degree rolls bring the aircraft back to its upright position

Now I look at you, my first boyfriend in college, and I think to myself, I'm afraid to have sex with you because "nice girls don't." You and I make out and come close to going all the way. You say you love me—and I believe it—you proposed; it thrilled me, and I hugged you, but I didn't say anything. I didn't feel ready to get married.

And now, months after your proposal, you say, "I think it's time we take our relationship to a deeper level." I don't know what you mean. I think we're already pretty close.

We enjoyed a pancake breakfast in a wide, sunny field before the airshow, and then the pilots did loops, rolls, and spins in the clear, blue sky. I could never be a stunt pilot. I don't trust my reflexes or ability to make quick decisions. And I'm afraid of heights, going fast, doing something stupid, losing control, and getting hurt.

You tell me, "He's going to do a Hammerhead Stall."

A Hammerhead Stall is a supreme vote of confidence in the universe and your own abilities—and an extraordinary gamble. We watch in awe as the pilot flies a small, single engine plane right up the side of the sky until it's pointed straight into heaven.

The speed decays, the motor hesitates and stalls. The pilot applies full rudder, rotates the plane, levels off, and it falls back toward earth, silently, its nose pointing straight at the ground.

There's a silence like death over the countryside. The small plane continues to drop, a stone through clouds.

Spectators listen for the engine. Anxious, I press against you.

The plane drops faster, gathers speed. It's been quiet too long. Way too long. The crowd stirs nervously. Start the engine now or you're done for. "What's wrong?" someone cries. No one answers.

The plane is too close to the ground. He'll never pull out of this. What if he gets killed? Pilots have died performing this maneuver. I've seen crashes on TV.

What if we're in the way? What if *we* get hit and killed?

The small plane disappears behind the tree line. I brace for the sickening crash, billowing smoke, flames. But wait, there it is, the clear, definite drone of an engine cutting through the crisp morning air—declaring survival. *Ahhh.* The pilot and plane rise upward, the crowd cheers, he does some fancy rolls to show off and then flies upside down for a while before leveling off.

The terrible suspense of a Hammerhead Stall is like being in love for the first time, I rest my head on your shoulder, you kiss my hair—your lips make soft, whispery sounds—and I find there in your arms a new kind of comfort and a new reason to be confused. You love me—but what if you knew about the turmoil that's my family and why I'm so cautious and socially anxious. You don't know that I'm scared all the time, scared of love, scared of my own demanding body and yours, afraid to let go and fall in love and trust myself, afraid to trust the universe and trust others. You draw me close; I lean into the curve of your arms. Do I dare hope that someone has finally come along to stop the terrible momentum of my loneliness?

The pilot executes another breath-taking Hammerhead Stall, hangs like an ornament in the brilliant sky, rotates, then levels off and falls downward in silence toward the earth. And I realize with clarity that it's me up there, performing a terrifying solo flight.

~~~

Back at your apartment after the airshow, you trace your fingers along my cheek and whisper, "I could love you so well if only you'd help me." I shift away from you on the couch. You say, "It's hard to be close to you. You keep things to yourself."

I don't know how to be open with someone. In high school, I was so apathetic and emotionally blunted that depression was a step up; I was happy to feel depressed, just happy to feel anything. I told Mom that I had trouble getting close to guys and she asked if it was because she wasn't close to Dad. I won't ask either her or Dad's relationship advice. If only someone would give me a formula for being well adjusted. I was never given the formula; some people got it, but not me.

"I'm sorry," I say, "I was raised by wolves."

"Even wolves bond with each other."

Attempting a bit of humor, I quip, "You've been reading *National Geographic*." You sigh and look sad.

I feel desperate and vulnerable. Dad told me that men only want two things: money or sex and, if I'm unlucky enough, they'll take both. He said that people are pigs. I don't want to believe him, but some part of me must. If people are so awful, why would anyone ever want to get close to them or even be one of them?

"I'm sorry. I'm just nervous a lot of the time." You draw me into an embrace. Yes, I want you. And I'm sure that the wanting is as intense as I imagine the final act will be.

"Come here," you pat the sleeping bag next to you. We're helping a friend of yours move to a new apartment and just brought over a carload of boxes. Other than that, the place is empty. Your friend is coming over later. I join you on the sleeping bag in the middle of the living room on the shiny hardwood floor.

You stroke my neck and move your hand to my breast. I don't object because I've let you do it before. You kiss me, I feel the moist, inner lining of your lips, the tip of your tongue a tentative question. You unfasten the top button of my blouse.

Just the top button; it is warm in here. And the second.

You unfasten the third button and fourth. I grasp the front of your shirt, push you away and hold on at the same time.

The last button; I'll just let you look. You unclasp my bra; the air cool against my breasts. "You're so beautiful."

After all this time, it happens so fast, your hands are everywhere, the weight of your body against me is strangely comforting as you kiss me in a deeper, more insistent way.

"Let me," you whisper.

So I do.

It turns out that a Hammerhead Stall isn't so much a stall as it's a hesitation and then a change in direction. Like any experienced pilot, if we keep our wits about us, we can pull out of a death-defying dive and land safely.

Sex was different than I expected, not as hot as making out. And afterward, a smear of blood on a piece of tissue. "I was a virgin," I inform you to which you reply, "I know."

Maybe there's a learning curve to having sex, so I'm back to where I started, reluctant, and you're back to trying to convince me, and I give in again. We go on like this for months. I didn't accept your marriage proposal—my parents' marriage was a disaster—and I have more to do before I settle down.

Then one day, you say, "I think we should see other people."

I'm stunned. "What's her name?" I want to know the name of my replacement.

You shake your head, "I'm not going to say, you're never going to meet her."

Eyes closed, I slump against your shoulder; I see a name in my mind, Barbara. "Is her name Barbara?"

The color drains from your face, you nod, and then, "See if you can guess her last name." I shake my head, speechless. I'm crying.

~~~

After six months of agonizing over losing you, I start to date again just as you come back, your affair ended. We date a couple more years, but not exclusively.

One day, after not having seen each other for several weeks, you come over. You're different, reserved, unavailable emotionally. You're not mine, you're someone else's. "Are you married?"

You close your eyes, nod, "Yes. She's pregnant."

And that's the end of that.

16. The Press Box

I sting with life. — Anne Sexton

I've lived most of my life, so far, outside my body, numb, apathetic, and afraid to trust. Now I step into long leg bones, slip into taut, hungry skin. Awaken and stretch. Sniff the wind. I want you.

You were a reporter for the Associated Press who loved me next and whom I loved fiercely in return. We sat in the Press Box (at University of Michigan football games), a working area reserved for the media, writers, and broadcasters. You said, "We're not supposed to cheer, it's a *working* press box. If you show favoritism for either team, security will haul you out of here." It was eerily quiet in the Press Box and I felt quite special to be there with you.

You were sexy, had a quick wit, a ready laugh, loved Pepsi, and were a talented writer; you won a prestigious journalism award.

In the Press Box, you wrote two endings for each sports story, the first in which the Michigan Wolverines won and, the other, in which they lost; that way you could get the story in to your editor faster and beat the deadline.

We went back to your place after you turned your story in—the story always took precedent, which I understood, being a writer myself—and we made love and listened to Simon and Garfunkel sing "Bridge Over Troubled Water."

We also made love in my dad's small boat on the Detroit River, which I thought was poetic justice for the emotional trauma he caused me over the years.

You and I couldn't get enough of each other. How could I have gone from being completely repressed with my first boyfriend to so over the top with you? It's like I was possessed. We did it just about everywhere for a year (except in the Press Box, of course, and you wouldn't do it in a snow drift, even though I tried to convince you otherwise, just for the experience).

You fed my skin hunger, felt so good in my arms, and asked if I ever thought about marriage—but I wanted adventure, and it turns out that you were still seeing your ex-fiancée, so I moved to San Francisco for the first time. I'd seen the city on a family vacation when I was 16, fell in love with it, and vowed to live there some day. I shared an apartment with three other women on Ninth Avenue and Judah Street where the streetcar turns around. We could see the ocean from our living room.

I tried to find work as a teacher, but my heart wasn't in it, there weren't any jobs to be found, and you kept sending me love letters, so I moved back to Michigan after six months, ready for you again, but while I was gone (neither of us knew if I was coming back), you proposed to someone else, abandoning both your ex-fiancée and me.

I listened to Jefferson Airplane's wistful song, "Coming Back to Me," and I cried, you were mine, mine, *mine*!

True to your profession, you wrote two endings for the story—for *our* story—one in which we ended up together and, the other, in which we did not.

17. The Mortician's Nightmare

It was a dark and stormy nightmare. — Neil Gaiman

Formaldehyde: a probable carcinogen. People who work with cadavers are exposed to a variety of hazardous materials including fumes and bodily fluids. The Occupational Safety and Health Administration states that exposure to formaldehyde might be associated with cancers of the lung, brain, and bone marrow. In spite of this, each year the funeral industry buries 350 thousand gallons of formaldehyde.

Hexachlorophene: cardiovascular toxicant. Exposure can contribute to a variety of diseases, including high blood pressure, hardening of the arteries, abnormal heartbeat, and decreased blood flow to the heart.

Formaldehyde and Hexachlorophene are neurotoxins, which can cause confusion, fatigue, and irritability. Toxins have also been implicated in "Intermittent Explosive Disorder" behavior.

Was Dad's job poisoning him? Were neurotoxins partly to blame for his rages? Uncle Don tells me "I watch your Dad embalm occasionally; sometimes he wears a mask and gloves, but more often not. He'll eat a sandwich with one hand and embalm with the other."

In addition to the health hazards of Dad's profession, and an unhappy marriage, add the emotional baggage from his childhood—a critical, emotionally distant mother, Hazel, who was said to have laughed and turned away when he asked for a hug. Hazel's own story was a disaster. Her mother read an article about men building a railroad in Canada who wanted pen pals; she wrote to one of them,

Loren, and signed Hazel's name. Hazel was unsophisticated, but her mother was cultured and loved to discuss literature. She (writing as Hazel) and Loren fell in love; he proposed. He and the real Hazel met a week before the wedding, and she liked him enough to marry him and kept the secret that it was her mother who wrote to him. He didn't suspect the bait-and-switch ruse or maybe lied to himself because the truth was unthinkable. He and Hazel married, then divorced. She married someone else, divorced him, married Loren again, and divorced again. A cousin said that they beat the kids.

Dad doesn't drink or do drugs, and isn't physically violent, but does have those outbursts of rage. Some nights he moves quietly, sleepwalking through the house stalking imaginary intruders. Once he exclaimed frantically to Mom, "Look out, he's got a gun!" The next day he said he didn't remember any of that.

My bedroom had a shuttered door that didn't lock. I sat in bed, watchful and on guard, as my father, a large, unhappy man moved through the house in his sleep, his psyche uncensored.

~~~

Dad remarries a cheerful woman named Margaret who tells me, "I'm bringing him back from the devastation of his marriage to your mom with plenty of love and good sex. He's starting to respond."

I like her a lot, but I doubt if Dad can ever be truly happy.

One of the funeral homes has a watchdog, a Doberman. Dad tells me, "I dreamed that I caught the dog chewing on a body's head."

I study him: a workaholic, sleep deprived, alternately full of rage and impenetrable silences, unapproachable and unavoidable, tormented and tormenting, and I wonder, what would it be like if you were dead? I'd be free. The thought startles me. Where'd it come from? What does it mean? Be careful of the questions you ask; the Universe answers.

18. Achy Breaky Heart

> There is a sacredness in tears. They are not the mark of weakness, but of power. They speak more eloquently than ten thousand tongues. They are messengers of overwhelming grief and unspeakable love. — Washington Irving

I'm tired of Dad telling me that the world is dangerous, and people are awful and can't be trusted. I want to believe that the world is a wonderful place full of adventure, fascinating people, and opportunities, so I'm thrilled to receive this in the mail from San Francisco State:

> I'm happy to tell you that you have been accepted into our graduate program based on the evaluation of your manuscript. Please check with the Registrar and bookstore before the beginning of the semester for information about registration procedures and scheduling classes. Welcome to San Francisco State Department of Creative Writing.

San Francisco State is one of only two universities (so far) in the entire country that offers an advanced degree in creative writing (the other is in Iowa), and they're only taking *one-eighth* of the applicants. That's five times that I've been recognized: I got into advanced English in high school, won honorable mention in the Scholastic Writing Awards, was sent to a week-long journalism conference at Columbia University, received seven years of standing scholarships to the elite Cranbrook Writers' Conferences, and now I've been accepted into a prestigious writing program. People must see something in me that Dad doesn't. Didn't he ever see it?

San Francisco is so far away! I'll leave the last week in July, drive cross-country, find an apartment when I get there, settle in, start classes, meet smart, fascinating people, and do what I really want to do: write! I go to bed laughing, wired, and exhilarated.

~~~

Mom is happy for me. Now to break the news to Dad who told me once that, "A girl should be a teacher or a nurse—or I'll send you to mortuary school if you want. I'll pay your way through college if you chose one of those professions."

I said, "Great, I can work with little kids, sick kids, or dead kids. I guess I'll be a teacher."

"Really?" he exclaimed. "Teaching doesn't pay much, and you don't have a brain for algebra, which you need for college. I think you should take Latin in school and become a medical secretary."

"Teaching it is," I said stubbornly.

So, I got an elementary-teaching degree (dad paid for it), and a master's degree in reading education for which I paid. I taught fifth grade for two years and then abandoned teaching to be a writer, which is what I wanted all along.

San Francisco will be a fresh start, no one knows me, I can be anyone I want to be, make a new life, and I'm going there a winner: the creative-writing program that accepted me is very hard to get into and nearly impossible if it's for a second master's degree.

Dad will probably give me grief about moving; that's why I waited until now to tell him, the day before I leave. I'm here in Berkley to tell him in person. "I've been accepted into the creative writing program at San Francisco State. They're only taking one-eighth of the applicants, so it's amazing that I got in. I'm moving to California tomorrow. I'm here to get my stuff from the attic. I'll stay at my apartment in Ann Arbor tonight, turn in the key in the morning, and be on my way."

He surprises me with silence, instead of a tirade, and then says, "I don't want you to move to San Francisco. The white slave traders will get you."

"At least it'll be steady work," I quip.

So, he protests my moving, but helps me load my car with things I've stored in the attic. It's a sweltering day, July 22. There's a lot of heavy lifting and he's out of shape. We go up and down the narrow attic stairs, the kind that pull down from the ceiling. I'm taking winter clothes that I had in storage, stories I wrote when I was a kid, my beautiful wooden clarinet, diaries, photo albums, and a cedar chest that we secured to the top of my car.

Dad and I work in silence, and then he walks me to my car and stands by the door before I drive away. "Do you love me?" he asks.

"In a way."

"That's what your mother says." He looks heavy and dejected. "Well, I love you," he says, and walks away.

I watch him go, simply a dad who just said good-bye to his child. He's wearing black pants and a blue, short-sleeved shirt. I feel an urge to jump out of the car and run to him, but what would I do? We never hug each other, and I wouldn't know what to say, so I decide to write to him when I get to San Francisco and settled in. I'll sort through all my complicated feelings and write him a letter. So, instead of following him, I drive away to spend the last night in my apartment in Ann Arbor before leaving for San Francisco.

The next morning, the phone rings. "Hello."

Margaret cries out, "Your father's dead!"

I collapse against the wall, regain my balance without falling.

"He had a heart attack!"

19. Knock, Knock, Who's There?

> One need not be a chamber to be haunted, one need
> not be a house, the brain has corridors surpassing
> material place. — Emily Dickinson

> Houses aren't haunted, people are.

Margaret meets me at the door when I come home to Berkley, from my apartment in Ann Arbor, for the funeral. Her face is streaked with tears, her lips swollen and bruised, "He didn't look well at breakfast. He leaned forward a little and then sat up again and said, 'I'm okay now.' That was the last thing he said. I gave him mouth-to-mouth resuscitation and I was yelling, 'Doug, you can't leave me, don't leave me!'"

~~~

I want to be alone the night before the funeral; my brothers and Margaret's son and daughter are in the house, so she lets me sleep in the "fifth-wheel" in the driveway. It's a luxury RV so large that you need a truck to pull it. Dad and Margaret, married just nine months, bought it to take on vacations. They used it once.

Knock, knock.

I bolt upright in bed. Is it someone from the house coming to talk?

Whoever knocked must have left, maybe thinking I wanted my privacy, but then *knock*, one rap on the back end of the trailer. Why would someone go back there and knock on the wall? *Knock.* I pull the sheet up to my chin. A little later *knock knock*, this time on the roof.

I'm weak with fright. Are the neighbor kids trying to scare me? No, I would have heard them climb the ladder on the side of the trailer and walk across the roof. It's not kids. Besides, they have short attention spans. They wouldn't knock randomly all night long, all over the trailer; they'd give themselves away, giggling like naughty children do.

Tree branches? No, branches scrape, they don't knock like that, and besides, there aren't any branches touching the trailer—Dad made sure of that when he parked it in the driveway. He didn't want it scratched. And there isn't any wind. The night is so quiet.

The trailer "settling" like a house settles, materials expanding and contracting with heat, cold, and humidity—*creak, snap, crack*? No, these sounds are different. Random knocking continues throughout the night, a mindless knocking on the sides of the trailer, the door, the roof. Sometimes it's one rap, sometimes *knock knock*.

Is Dad trying to reach me one last time? No, he's in the funeral home, embalmed for the viewing and waiting to be cremated. But what if he's out floating around somewhere—an unattached cluster, separated from his body—like the man Dad embalmed whom he thought might have still been alive? Oh, God, I'm scared. I don't know what to do, as always where Dad is concerned.

I was never prepared as a child to hear what scared him the most, to hear the horror stories he told. I couldn't deal with being his confidant. I didn't know how to help. I felt inadequate and didn't feel safe around him; not since the incident in the lake when I was six years old. If I cling to him, he'll go under with me on his back.

And, yet, had he been clinging to me, maybe thinking "You're leaving me? Well, I'm going to die, then."

But, Dad, you have a new wife. It's time for me to go live my own life, now, in San Francisco.

I cover my head with the sheet despite the sweltering summer heat. My face is oily with sweat, my skin sticky and salty. I could open the door and look out, but it's three in the morning and there wouldn't be anyone there—or maybe *he'd* be there. I make a low, terrified humming sound. Of course, he'd come to me, if it were possible, like he turned to me in life when he was disturbed, and as usual, there's nothing I can do.

~~~

The viewing, the night before the funeral, is at Kingsley-Barrett Funeral Home. Dan Barrett meets me at the door and reaches to give me a consoling hug. I twist away. Nobody touch me, nobody!

"I'm so sorry about your father," he says. "I loved your dad. I embalmed him and cried all the way through it."

He looks pale and exhausted. He was the one who became a partner in the funeral home instead of Dad. Dad's friend and one-time "rival" embalmed him, and it was on the house—no charge.

A little later Dan tells me, "We're late bringing the body in. Your dad was too tall for the casket, so we had to find another one."

Margaret tries to prepare me emotionally to see Dad for the first time in the casket. "It'll be like nothing you've ever experienced. You'll remember it for the rest of your life."

She should know. She buried her first husband. Dad's her second.

Dan appears again, "Your Dad's ready for viewing."

I approach the casket. Dad told me that sometimes people are surprised when they see the embalmed body of a friend or a relative for the first time and they exclaim, "He looks just like himself."

Well, Dad looks just like himself, dressed in the deep maroon jacket and the dark pants he was wearing when he and Margaret got married. He's wearing his glasses and Masonic ring. I feel numb.

I take a seat in the chapel behind a curtain that gives the family some privacy. The Masonic service has metaphysical overtones, which surprises and pleases me. Was Dad interested in metaphysics?

After the service, Uncle Don takes us out to eat and tells the server, "These kids just lost their father, keep the drinks coming."

I don't eat or drink anything. Over the next two weeks I lose 10 pounds.

~~~

Margaret kept the fifth-wheel luxury RV, the car, the house, and Dad's personal items. She gave each of us three kids a thousand dollars, "There isn't more because the funeral expense ate up most of the insurance policy" (even though the embalming was free), "and I used some of the money to pay your mom for her share of what she put into buying the house in Berkley."

One of my brothers took Dad's guns.

I didn't think I took anything, but when I got to San Francisco and opened the cedar chest, I saw Dad's trocar, the embalming instrument that he used to pierce bloated organs. I don't remember taking it. Where would I even have found it? Surely no one gave it to me. Who put it in the cedar chest?

20. The Fire Underneath

Look and you will find it. What is unsought is undetected.
— Sophocles

"Did you ever see a psychologist?" a friend asks.

"No, I write; that's my therapy. But I did see a student in a psychology-graduate program for a few months; I was his coursework, maybe his thesis."

The first thing I told him was, "I can't seem to get happy." He nodded and didn't say anything. I should have bailed out immediately. Turns out, he was of the school of thought: sit there silently and let me do the talking, free associate or something. I came from silence, from people who didn't talk about their feelings, so it galled me to have him (with all his supposed knowledge of human behavior, which might have helped me had he shared it with me) sit there, session after session, and say virtually nothing, although he did point out that "When other people make mistakes, you get hurt."

That made sense. I figured that if I were smart, vigilant, and cautious as could be, I wouldn't get hurt or killed, but I also needed *everyone else* to be predictable, reliable, and incapable of making mistakes, so I wouldn't get hurt or killed. I chose my (few) friends carefully, but there were things I couldn't avoid or control:

- In second grade being falsely accused. During recess we weren't supposed to look in the windows of the first-floor classrooms because it'd disturb the kids inside in class. I walked by a little blonde girl who had her hands on the brick ledge, peering into a classroom. My teacher came out, demanded to know who was looking in the window, the guilty little girl—the real culprit—pointed at me, the teacher came over and slapped me hard across the face. I was stunned. Any teacher would have been lucky to have

me in class. I got good grades and was quiet and well behaved. Never any trouble. And she hit me. Mrs. Everett—I'll always remember her name.
- In sixth grade, a toboggan accident because the girl in front leaned the wrong way, tipped us over, and I was dragged down the icy hill on my face; it scraped the skin off my face and gave me a black eye (my glasses twisted, but probably saved my eye). When the scab fell off eventually, I put it in my diary next to the tear-stained note that my dog died. I saved tears and scabs; how theatrical and, somehow, touching.
- When I was older, bitten in the butt by a Bull Mastiff that a neighbor let run loose. It didn't leave a mark; the dog was just trying to intimidate me—mission accomplished.
- When I was older, two serious traffic accidents, my cars totaled, someone else's fault each time.

There were many more times when nothing happened, of course, neighbors kept their dogs in the yard and teachers were inspiring instead of punitive, but again, I let exceptions become the rule. I became hypervigilant, withdrawn, self-protective, and on guard against the unexpected.

I got tired of the student psychologist and his silences, so I stopped seeing him and wrote this book instead (writing saves and serves me). I wrote that after being strong my entire childhood, and holding it all together year after year, after Dad calling me "stupid" when I wasn't, after all the bodies, all the pickups and deliveries, the firecrackers exploding behind me in the living room, the dunking in the lake, the casket in the living room, a little boy hacked to death, chasing ambulances, the trip to the insane asylum, after Dad's horrific, kitchen-table confession, and my mom being my rock through it all—the one who fostered in me a love of reading and writing, who was leader of my Girl Scout troop, whom I admired for her strength throughout a difficult marriage—she stopped noticing me and turned her attention away; that's when it all came apart, when I came apart and forgot my past. I experienced a fugue state—temporary amnesia—when I finally admitted to myself that what Dad said about her was true, even though she still hadn't admitted it (not that women loving women is a bad thing, I just didn't want my mom to be in love with one when I was a kid in the late 1950s).

I remember learning about muck fires when I visited Harrison's farm. Muck fires can burn underground, silently and unnoticed for months, sometimes years, and suddenly topple a tree—which can fall on someone—a mile away.

Mom was there for me, always predictable—until she wasn't—until she ran away from home to be with Janine. It was my mother, my *mother; she* was the fire underneath.

INTO THE WILD DIVIDE

21. You, You, You, and You

> Last night you were unhinged like some desperate,
> howling demon. You frightened me. Do it again.
> — Morticia Addams

And now I want you, you, you, and you. There were so many of you.

You were a professor with an IQ that rivaled Einstein's who told me that I was a genius. And you were another professor who knew I was seeing other men and declared adamantly, "No one will ever love you like I do!"

You were a law student, you were a philosopher who lived in a farmhouse and owned horses (we rode together, galloped, me sitting in front of you), you were the one in the arboretum/mineral baths/at a wedding, you owned a bulldog/worked with migrant workers/ran adult education classes. You, you, you, and you, here I come, ready or not.

You were an artist who chanted in the shower, spray painted your old car silver to glow in the dark, took me to the zoo, park, beach, museum, and fed me fish and chips before bed.

You were a high school teacher. You were a musician who played an autoharp. You were the president of a Karate club who did pushups on your knuckles—you deliberately had the nerves severed in your hands so you wouldn't feel the pain, your knuckles permanently swollen and calloused—could you feel me?

You were a "psychic," medieval looking with shoulder-length hair and a hint of a Roman nose. I believed in your "powers," but you taught me that mind reading isn't always real, sometimes it's an illusion, and sometimes relationships are based on patter.

You were someone whom women proposition after your Karate expositions; I watched you earn your second-degree black belt. Does it hurt to break boards with your forehead? You answered, "Only if the board doesn't break. Focus behind the board and aim for that spot." I drove 500 miles to seduce you. I kiss the small of your back, smooth, firm skin. You were well worth the drive.

You were a veterinarian student who owned a French-Alpine goat that tried to stand on top of the other animals on the farm because climbing was in the goat's genes.

You were an artist who marveled "I didn't know a man could have multiple orgasms."

You worked for the CIA, then became an executive in a mining company, and lived in a lovely home in the Sausalito Hills. We're sitting in a bar and the song "McArthur Park" comes on. I say, "Listen for the part that says, 'After all the loves of my life I'll be thinking of you and wondering why,' and look around at everyone in the bar remembering that one love." I glance around the room, and then back at you—you're looking directly at me with a smile, looking to see me remembering the one love of my life, or am I the one love of yours?

All the stylized love scenes on TV and in the movies: candles and flowers, rose petals strewn across the floor and mattress, lovers falling in slow motion onto the bed (or he carries her to the bed; can't she walk?), the camera panning to flames in the fireplace, cutting to commercial, and afterwards they lie in bed talking. It's not really like that, is it? Was I doing it wrong? It's doing it on the living room couch because the bedroom is too far away, doing it leaning against a wall, holding onto the end of a dock in a lake at night, laughing like kids exhilarated and exhausted in the bathtub.

It's losing count, having whomever I want, whenever; breathing shallow, then dizzy and deep, losing my breath, and then, release.

People who advocate abstinence must have libidos that idle on low or none. What a disservice they do teenagers to offer abstinence as the only method of birth control. Maybe they've never lost control, never come unhinged. I've come unhinged.

I live near the infamous Haight-Ashbury district; I moved in after the "Summer of Love," but the air is still full of permission. What freedom, to have whomever I want. There's a (bedroom) window of opportunity; I climb through. I still have a lot more "go" in me.

You paid half my plane fare from San Francisco back to Michigan, hoping to convince me to stay.

You came to Michigan from San Francisco hoping to convince me to return.

You fed me grilled steak and salad and made vodka gimlets, we swam in the dark lake at night and reached for each other through the silky water, you had color-coordinated bedding—printed sheets and pillowcases that matched—too expensive for me to afford.

I live in the wild divide between the earth and the gods, and you live in the wild divide of me. I stretch, proud of my height, and take up space; I sit in jeans, legs spread casually like a man sits. I'm here, intellect blazing, body craving, addicted to the idea of you. I sting with life, with the fierce immediacy of it and with immense gratitude for having been given a life (my parents wanted children, but not so soon, I surprised them; I rushed to get here).

I was the mortician's child who grew up surrounded by death. I felt powerless, apathetic, and unreal. Now that I'm in college and away from home, I want life! I'm in charge. I make the choices. Having sex makes me feel alive. I don't think about mundane things like buying bread or milk, the price of gas, dirty dishes, or what to cook for dinner; I just want you, you, you, and you; my need, your good fortune.

22. Hunger for the Vivid

What more could you ask for than life itself?
— Stan Rice

San Francisco State University, two weeks after Dad's funeral, I'm taking a poetry class from a vampire; or rather, from Stan Rice. His wife, Anne Rice, is said to be modeling a vampire after him in a book she's writing, *Interview with the Vampire*. She says in an interview, "My beautiful husband Stan was the inspiration for the vampire Lestat. It was Stan's blue eyes and feline grace that inspired Lestat's charm and magnetism and mesmerizing movement."

Stan paces, slim and animated, in front of the class. I suspect grief fuels much of his creative fervor as he tries to come to terms with the agonizing loss of their little girl, Michelle, almost six years old, dead of leukemia. He searches for something precise on which to depend, muses out loud to himself for us to hear and learn, "I was working on a poem, trying to find the right word—did the fish nibble the surface of the water? No, the word 'nibble' isn't exact enough."

I thought "nibble" was a great word; now I'm worried, what if I'm not exact enough? Poetry is so unforgiving in its attempt to be universal and true in all places for all people.

Stan speaks about a "hunger for the vivid." In his book, *Some Lamb,* he writes that God "got hungry and needed some silverware so he opened/My daughter and he said, Look at this here little faceful of bones …" I shudder. She was opened like a silverware drawer and consumed as though she were a succulent piece of lamb.

I sit in the student union at a corner table slumped over the book, head bowed—face hidden by my thick hair—crying. Stan's poetry is fierce and intimate; it shakes me, there's nowhere to run, fresh in from the death of my father.

I'll make something of everything and meaning from nothing; my life *will* make sense. I scatter books throughout my apartment so whatever room I'm in there'll be a book to read—physics, poetry, philosophy, astronomy, psychology—for my unconscious mind to sift through and glean metaphors, healing, surprising connections. Bookmarkers advance steadily through all the books. My brain never rests, I'm hyper, frantic; I want to absorb information even faster, so I learn to speed read.

I suspect there's something underlying life, maybe the unified field for which Einstein searched. But what ties everything together, what's the common denominator? I'm with Einstein who wanted nothing less than "to understand the mind of God."

That night I go to bed and fall into a troubled sleep. I awaken, turn my head toward the closet, look *down* at the doorknob, but I usually look *up* from my bed at the doorknob. Have I been sleeping in layers, astral and physical, with a space in between? I lower myself gently back into my body.

~~~

I choose three authors to study for my master's degree: Anne Sexton, Lawrence Durrell, and Wallace Stevens.

Sexton, a confessional poet—who writes about adultery and abortion—had a couple nervous breakdowns and many affairs. She was diagnosed with bipolar disorder and then hysteria because she mimicked—either intentionally or unconsciously—the various mental illnesses of her fellow patients in the asylum. Her therapist encouraged her to take up poetry; she wrote the first draft of *The Awful Rowing Toward God* in 20 days.

Durrell writes about relativity in *The Alexander Quartet*, four novels, each of which presents one of four characters' perspectives of a single set of events. Reality isn't absolute; we each create our own reality by the way we interpret the circumstances in our lives.

Stevens, who's also an attorney and insurance salesman, sees poetry as a product of the imagination, which shapes the world; reality is an activity that we piece together like a puzzle to try to find meaning to our lives.

Sexton, Durrell, Stevens. I have every aspect of myself covered—angst and intellect—and, as I study each of them to meet the requirements of my master's degree, they each help to shape me.

~~~

Another night I awaken standing by my desk, "Clutter everywhere, what a mess." I look down and I'm not there, I turn and, terrified, run through the wall—it tugs at me as I break through—run into the hall screaming for my roommate, but I don't have vocal cords, my throat is cottony, no sound comes out. I see that my roommate isn't home—her bedroom door ajar, her room dark.

Awake now, back in bed, I sit up slowly, shaken. I go check her room for real; she's not there, her door ajar, room dark—just the way I saw it.

My brain isn't weaving information together from my senses—there's something wrong with it—my senses hike out on their own in different directions, vision goes one way, hearing another. Touch tells me that I'm lying down, vision tells me I'm in the hall. Humpty Dumpty sat on a wall, Humpty Dumpty had a great fall, and all the king's horses and all the king's men couldn't put Humpty together again.

My dreams leave my brain at night and march and waltz across the room; I can watch them outside of myself. My unconscious mind speaks up mostly at night. I see "ghosts," flashes of light, earthworms dropping out of the picture in my bedroom (I pull the bed away from the wall so the worms drop onto the floor rather than onto my pillow). Is this some sort of strange dream/waking phenomena on the threshold of sleep? What's going on? The images don't interfere with my studies during the day or with my job.

But occasionally during the day, I *sense* things, like the young man sitting in front of me on the bus. He's clearly "on something" or maybe he's schizophrenic; laughing to himself. What's he seeing? I wonder, and then boom, I'm in a bottomless pit with cold, black flames licking at me, I give a start, he sits up straight, rigid, turns around to look at me in surprise, and then bursts out laughing, delighted to discover someone else in the pit with him.

~~~

The artist M.C. Escher painted a series of staircases, ascending and descending in infinite loops. He stated, "I don't use drugs, my dreams are frightening enough." Mine, too. As long as I can remember, I've dreamed of staircases, each one terrifying and unique. Something prevents me every time from going up or down: halfway to my destination, the stairs turn upside down and I must defy gravity to keep from falling off, or the staircase stops on the edge of a chasm and continues on the other side—too far for me to jump. I suspect that my waking life is structured unconsciously by unpredictable, unmanageable staircases.

I'm coming apart like Italian artist Piero Fornasetti's painting of a woman's face unwinding in a spiral. I use intellect as ballast for my emotions. I scribble possibilities across a piece of paper and try to figure out what's wrong with me: epilepsy, psychic, psychotic break, post-traumatic stress.

Does my embattled brain-state have to do with having been a mortician's child, on high alert most of the time; hypervigilant, my senses, outer and inner, so exaggerated that they respond to activity below most people's conscious awareness? I can't control it. Much like my life.

I don't make left turns in the car, they make me feel vulnerable and I don't trust my senses or reflexes—right turns form neat, tight squares like I'm hugging myself. When I left home and came to California, I was done being yelled at; I didn't deserve that growing up and won't ever put up with it again. My anger keeps people at a distance. I know all I need to know; no one can contribute anything to my life—I won't let them. I detest asking for information or help, and when people try to help of their own accord rather than wait for me to ask, I don't trust their motives. Leave me alone. Don't watch me. Go away.

My psyche whirls: pureed, chopped, and liquefied. The standard emotions—happy, sad, mad, glad—aren't enough to deal with my life. There are intense emotions beyond anger and grief—that exist at cellular levels—that come over me like seizures and immobilize me with anxiety, tunnel vision, and irrational thoughts. To feel simple anger or grief would be such a relief.

See, I have a compass; I carry it in my purse because directions mean nothing to me and sometimes, I must go places. I can still get lost with a compass and a map.

I bring home one of the other students from class, nice looking with long hair down past his shoulders, and powerful in bed. Having sex grounds me. It's immediate and intense, the only time my senses align themselves. I don't mind an occasional, inadvertent bruise.

And every now and then, *kapow*! I'm a lightning rod for God—like that time in church when I was 15—instantly without warning I become the cosmic sea, transcendent and blissful, fluid and floating. When you can get God like that, who needs the slow dribble of religion?

~~~

Dad didn't want me to go to San Francisco, and maybe died to make his point, but I came anyway—or, at least, part of me; the rest still has to catch up. As I turn the pages of *Interview with the Vampire,* I detect echoes of the loss of a little girl, Michelle Rice. Life feeds on us and turns us, slowly day by day, over to eternal life. I put *Interview with the Vampire* on the shelf next to *Some Lamb*. What art will grief make of my experiences?

~~~

I search for the Life behind life. I'm primitive, instinctual. Everything is brighter, faster, louder, slower than it used to be. The wind blows through me, stars glitter inside me. I'm transparent, waiting to be filled. San Francisco sparkles at night, an exciting wonderland, and not once does a white slave trader ever approach me as my father feared.

~~~

Writing is the way I exist in the world; being published validates my existence. But is it enough? Some writers receive critical acclaim and kill themselves, such as John Berryman, Hart Crane, Randall Jarrell, Sylvia Plath, Sarah Teasdale, Ernest Hemingway, and more than 70 others. Seventy! Is there pathology associated with writing; an unbearable tension, a pressure that builds, and then we *must* write? Writing has turned into an incurable "disease" for me with discomfort and discontent that can only be alleviated temporarily by massive infusions of metaphor—and being published.

What will become Stan Rice and his wife Anne with her freshly minted novel about vampires, and my fellow students: Frances Mayes, Michael Creedon, Frances Phillips, feminist poet Karen Brodine who writes about a woman lover, and Fredric Matteson who won a coveted Joseph Henry Jackson Award for a book of poetry.

One year into my master's degree program, Anne Sexton, the poet I was studying, who won the Pulitzer Prize for her book of poetry, *Live or Die,* locks herself in her garage, starts the engine of her car, and dies of carbon monoxide poisoning.

~~~

 The strange experiences happen at night during some sort of half-awake, half-asleep state? My mattress is on the floor because I didn't want to clean under it. Now I'm standing on the edge of it, my body rigid and tilted back at a 45-degree angle; another out-of-body experience? Am I "levitating"? I panic, but haven't fallen, so I relax into it and feel palms, one on each shoulder blade, righting me again so I'm standing up straight. I slowly lower myself to my knees like praying and then lie down.
 I turn on my side, press a pillow against my chest and solar plexus to keep my spirit in place.
 A couple months later, again in bed at night, "vibrations" move through my body, a gentle hum in my veins. With my blood purring in its channels, I step "out" and visit people.

> Turned inside out, I'm all center and no flesh, a phantom who glides through walls and slips into your home like air, I imagine you in the kitchen pouring orange juice, frowning, sensing me? On your table a fish swims in a crystal bowl, I settle into it, body gold and fin wet, a slow subtle drifting. The next day I tell you that I visited you and you scold, "Don't do that again, you fried my brain."

What power, to be invisible and mobile, to fly and float. Exhilarating. And then, in the night, I my arm rises up, stretches, it looks like my hand goes through the wall, dear God, I can't stay in my body! Have I become an unattached cluster like the "living" man Dad might have mistaken for dead and embalmed?

23. The Woman with No Pupils

I think it's in my basement. Let me go upstairs and check.
— M.C. Escher

To look into the heart is not enough … one must look into the cerebral cortex. — T.S. Elliott

Am I having a nervous breakdown? The disturbing nighttime experiences don't seem to interfere with what I need to do during the day, like going to work and classes, but I desperately want to figure out what's going on.

"You here for the brainwave study?" a technician asks at the Langley Porter Institute. I nod. They want to see if brainwaves differ according to the kinds of reading people do: short stories, scientific material, or poetry. I'm here to help with their research but have a hidden agenda. I want someone to look inside my head and tell me what's going on in there.

He attaches me to the EEG machine with electrodes stuck to my head and goes into another room. I sink into one of my "states," the one where I see vivid pictures inside the back of my brain, like there's a small room in there with a TV in it.

He comes in, perturbed, "Stop doing that, you're messing up the experiment." So, I'm not imagining that something weird is going on inside my head.

He exclaims, "You have the fastest brainwaves I've ever seen."

Hoping for a diagnosis I ask, "Epilepsy or genius?"

He disappoints me, "Individual differences."

I cross epilepsy off my list of suspicions. I don't want epilepsy, I just want to know something for certain. By the way, the experiment indicates that people go into alpha when they read poetry, and beta when they read fiction, non-fiction, and science.

~~~

I continue to have visions and walk through walls at night, seem to read people's thoughts, and hear voices (encouraging, instructive voices, never anything that tells me to hurt myself or others). I allude to this in letters home to family and friends. Mom asks, "Are you on drugs?" No, never have been, this happens naturally. I'm afraid of what might happen if I did do drugs.

I devour books like *The Haunted Mind, The Varieties of Religious Experience*, and *Psychoanalysis and the Occult*—looking for my "symptoms" and discover the following statement: "Psychic experiences are too much like the delusions of the mentally ill." Apparently, it's an occupational hazard for therapists to have patients with "psychic" abilities.

> The experiences disappear as people regain their balance … there's a phase of infancy characterized by omnipotence of thought and eventually regulated by 'reality' as most people know it, reality as a consensus of opinion … The personality under stress regresses to these infantile predispositions.

I try to tamp down my anxiety, but it comes out one way or another. My faculty advisor, Kathleen Fraser, reads my poems and exclaims, "It's like these were written by two different people."

Only two?

And my thesis advisor, Mark Linenthal, sets my work aside (in which I write about my experiences), "I think you had a psychotic break."

I disagree. I refuse to have a nervous breakdown because I'm afraid I wouldn't do it right, and I like to do things perfectly (Mom told me that she never had a breakdown because she couldn't afford it financially). So, I just keep "breaking" and having bizarre experiences for no apparent reason. To have a complete nervous breakdown might be a relief.

I'm feeling alone and isolated. I write a poem: I'm a woman with no pupils who sees with her elbows and forearms. Pupils are unnecessary, even dangerous; things would fall into my head if my eyes had holes. My skin serves me well, my palms are irises, and I'm alone because no one knows where to look to meet my gaze.

~~~

I avoid counselors and other mental health "experts" with the power to "put me away" like those people in the Pontiac Insane Asylum. I don't trust any of them to understand me. They might think I'm crazy, but I function perfectly well during the day, for the most part.

I keep writing poetry, have sex to ground myself, hold a job—first, editor of the SFSU School of Education's newsletter, and then assistant to the dean—pay my bills, study Sexton, Durrell, and Stevens, maintain a 3.9 grade point average (out of 4.0), and earn my second master's degree.

24. Séance, Late Afternoon

He who cannot pause to wonder is as good as dead.
— Albert Einstein

Margaret carried Dad's ashes to Dexter, Maine, to a cemetery where her family members will be buried, far from us and all that he loved, distrusted, and wanted; he is where dark pines know the truth, the real secret of shadows. He is new here, he is dead here—resigned, relieved, begin to trust the wind.

There was a lot between us that we left unsaid, so out of curiosity, I visit a spiritualist church, and schedule a séance.

Before the Séance

I sit on this side in the watery light waiting for Dad to come. I speak of "side" as if death lies in a certain direction, as if "past" were behind.

The spirit medium lights some incense. Cinnamon apple scent drifts upwards. I remember when I was a child standing in the arctic breath of a stone cider mill, close enough to see clots of moss growing on the huge, wet wheel, ponderous and rolling in place, carving the icy stream to ribbons to turn the presses to crush the apples to liquid. Men in high rubber boots run across the presses, push pulp into wooden troughs to be collected and crushed again. The air is thick with the fragrance of apples; I clutch one in my hand for an autumn picnic with parents I thought would never die. I bite the red crust, teeth declaring, "Dad, I assumed you would *be* forever." Like brittle beetles snap against the windshield on a family trip, my teeth crack the skin.

During the Séance

This small room, with its table, rug, lamps, and four walls, is a portal where I wait to speak of love with those on the "other side."

The medium says sternly, "If you've come to test me, you can leave right now."

"I'm not here to test you," I reply, incensed. Truth is I doubt that the séance is real, but a small part of me hopes it is.

He turns out the light. Darkness bolts me in. Absent-minded humming starts while I sit on a hard, green chair and, as instructed, say the Lord's Prayer to "raise the vibrations."

A disembodied voice calls down from the ceiling, "Give me the names of the spooks you want, and I'll go get them."

The word "spooks" seems disrespectful, but I comply and say my father's name.

The voice says, "While I'm gone, talk to this little girl."

The child—several feet from my knees, it seems—chats about independence and freedom. If I reach to touch the forbidden energy, would my fingers tangle in web? The medium warned, "If you touch me during the séance the ectoplasm will snap back into my solar plexus and electrocute me."

Does health insurance cover that?

I ask the little girl, "What's it like where you are?"

"It's beautiful. Everything is so clear. I can see so much more than I did when I was alive. Your father is here now."

I jerk, startled. Oh please, let it be.

"This is your father. I love you. I never showed you, I was afraid of spoiling you. I know now that I was wrong being so reserved."

I forget my rehearsed questions. My voice stumbles, "You made it hard for me to know that I loved you, too."

"Do you remember the yellow roses I gave you?"

"No. I remember that you gave me flowers with a Bird of Paradise in the middle—I had the measles."

"You just don't remember the yellow roses."

The Bird of Paradise was exquisite. It probably came from someone's funeral arrangement, but it was the thought that counted. When it wilted, I dissected it.

"Do you remember what a tomboy you were?" he asks.

"I remember wanting to be." I longed to feel at home in my body, to roller skate without fear and throw a ball like a boy, but I was a klutz, totally clumsy.

"Yes, you fell out of enough trees."

"I never fell out of any trees."

"You just don't remember."

I want to cry out, you wouldn't let me climb trees. I believed it when you said I'd fall and kill myself, don't be wrong about me, even now!

"I love you. Always remember that. Don't be like me, withholding your feelings."

"I won't," I lie (some anguish never dies).

After the Séance

I walk home in the late afternoon sun. A little girl, laughing, runs to her daddy, her tiny sandals smack the sidewalk, he smiles, his arms open wide to receive her. I blink back tears.

My needs went out, and having reached a distant edge, turned back on themselves, "straight ahead" always meaning "toward the center." The center is a hunger I keep coming back to. But terror is to reach that center, finally, and to find someone else there, no, to find everyone else there, no, a core of witches, those dark memories.

I look out my kitchen window, but at night the view bends in. I'm trying to see my neighborhood; instead, I see my own startled reflection looking back.

25. *Ahhh*, Chocolate!

Chocolate is nature's way of making up for Mondays. — Author Unknown

I felt really depressed today, so I ate a whole bunch of chocolate. It cheered me up quite a lot. Chocolate seems to be the answer. — Stephen King

Sometimes when I think back over the emotionally trying times in my life, I feel like eating chocolate. But no more nervous eating. I'm not going to binge on chocolate anymore. I mean it. I'm going to quit eating it starting right now. Mom might send brownies for my birthday or Christmas like I asked her to before I gave up chocolate, so if she does, I might just eat those to be polite, and then no more.

I haven't had chocolate now in, let's see, 60 minutes …. Okay, now it has been 77 minutes. I was never heavily into it, anyway, unlike some people who just can't stop eating it.

Occasionally I eat it, I mean, *ate* it to cheer myself up if I felt nervous, angry, or depressed. But what's to worry about these days? And remember, the word "binge" means a spree, something that happens occasionally. So, when people binge, they're inadvertently declaring, "I don't do this very often." What's real important is that I never purged. I haven't ever thrown up on purpose.

Sometimes I ate more chocolate depending on how my relationships were going. When I felt frustrated, I'd hide somewhere and eat chocolate. But I've changed for the better: I go for more walks, quit work earlier in the evenings, and eat healthy food. My kitchen has large glass jars full of lentils, brown rice, and all kinds of beans, pasta, and dried kelp.

What concerns me is depriving myself of something for the rest of my life. I could reserve chocolate for very special treats; nothing wrong with a little fudge if I haven't had any in five or six *months*. Knowing that I can *choose* to eat it removes the compulsion to eat it.

I'm in a bind being an inspirational writer—published frequently in Science of Mind magazine—who *should* set a good example, but who feels a little lousy sometimes. Life happens to me, too. I want to create a monster that becomes a classic, like Frankenstein's monster, or Dr. Jekyll and Mr. Hyde, or the Wolfman. Depending on my mood in the mornings, I either write psychological thrillers, horror stories, or inspirational articles.

Since I've given up chocolate, it's okay to eat one of the brownies—that I bought from the discount pastry shelf at the grocery store—as a reward for giving it up ... *Ahhh*, moist and chewy ... *ummm* ...

Now that I'm officially off chocolate, I can eat another brownie without guilt. I used to buy candy and ask my neighbor to keep it for me—she isn't a big chocolate fan (can you imagine?)—and I ate a couple pieces when I went to visit. That worked, but there was always the challenge of getting a new bag over to her house before I got into it. It's okay if other people eat chocolate. I don't judge them for that. And seeing them eat it doesn't tempt me in the least.

My friend Cyndi reads this and exclaims, "I love it. I can *sooo* relate. I'm planning to invite you over soon, and I better eat all the chocolate before you arrive; strictly for *your* sake, not that I'd want to eat any at all, but I'll make myself do it just to help you out."

Should I have told Dad sooner that I was going to San Francisco, so he'd be better prepared emotionally and maybe wouldn't have had separation anxiety? He was a heart attack waiting to happen—too much coffee, too many donuts, meals on the run, overweight and anxious, too little sleep, worried incessantly, high blood pressure, inhaled neurotoxins at work—but some part of me must have wondered if it was my decision to follow my dream of being a writer, instead of a teacher, nurse, or a mortician, that broke his heart.

As an adult, I marvel at my emotional resilience (although I do like, I mean, I *did* like a bit of chocolate every now and then).

I used to freeze candy, so it'd be too hard to eat, but then ate it frozen, like I was addicted, which I'm not. Too much of anything can be bad. Even vitamins can be toxic if you eat too many, but they're good in small amounts. Maybe I'll limit myself to finer, premium chocolate, like Godiva chocolate, for special occasions. *Ewww*, I feel queasy. I shouldn't have eaten so many brownies. There's still several left, though.

Dad's work took precedent over family. Going to the lake, his pager went off, he slammed on the brakes and turned the car around. Mom didn't drive at the time, so she couldn't take us. The needs of his clients came before his and ours. Was he angry that his trip to the lake was disrupted? Did he wonder if he was a good father?

Uncle Don told me, "Your dad and I were on the boat. He had a gun in his hand, he said 'my wife left me, and my kids hate me.' I talked him out of killing himself that day."

Dad lost his sense of smell; deadened by the fumes from embalming fluid and the odor of cadavers? Had he lost himself, as well? He saw people at their worst, quarreling, grieving, stressed out. Did he have secondary post-traumatic stress? Was he burned out?

Without death, Dad wouldn't have a job, and being a freelancer who worked for 22 funeral homes kept him very busy. Work became his life and, so, death became his life. He didn't drink or do drugs. He socialized with neighbors sometimes and belonged to several service clubs. He was also a Mason; I don't know much about Masons. I don't know if he had any close friends.

Did he have a poor self-concept and low self-esteem? Looking at a photo of himself once, he laughed uncomfortably, "Big ugly."

Whatever we had going on in our lives must have seemed trivial to him compared to what he saw at work every day, which probably caused him to lose perspective and empathy. He dealt with other people's grief, depression, trauma, and anxiety, so our problems must have seemed insignificant to him; you were chosen last for the dodge ball team in gym, big deal, at least you weren't hit by a car and killed. The next-door neighbor boy teased you on the way home from school and ripped up the picture you drew, so what, he didn't hack you to death. Your leg hurts; don't be a sissy, you're not dying.

Did he blame himself that Mom was in love with someone else? Did he feel that he let her down? Was he so numbed by death that he didn't know how to relate to us, didn't know how to get back to us or how to get us back?

I try to rationalize eating the brownies, which are made with all-natural ingredients: milk chocolate (milk's good), sugar (made from a plant), milk, cocoa butter, lecithin (an emulsifier that breaks down cocoa butter fat so it moves easily in smaller particles through the blood stream), and salt, which is okay if you have low blood pressure like I do. Just a small bite of brownie ... *ahhh* ... My body felt tight like it was going through withdrawal or something.

In public, Dad was charming, funny even, according to a cousin; in private, he was often scary angry. Had his life lost its meaning? Always on call, always near home in case a call comes in. He went to church for a while: Pentecostal, Baptist, Presbyterian. Mom found comfort in church, but he stopped going. His excuse? His pager might go off during the service and interrupt the sermon.

He was sick. He had a toxic family at home and neurotoxins at work. He needed help and didn't know where to turn.

Then there's Mom with challenges of her own. Her father, a widower, sent her and her younger sister from where the three of them lived on an idyllic Connecticut farm ("Joy Farm," a writers' haven, artist colony, and a spiritual retreat in the Litchfield Hills), to live with his strict, older sister, Elizabeth, who had a maid and a butler and a large home in Oshkosh, Wisconsin. He was trying to raise two daughters by himself and, as wrenchingly difficult as it was for him to part with them, he thought it was for their own good. According to his journal, after he put them on a train for Wisconsin, he went behind the station and threw up.

One day Mom overheard Aunt Elizabeth complain to someone that after having raised her own children, she now had to raise her brother's children.

Mom told me, "I felt like I'd been kicked in the stomach." But in fact, according to one of my cousins, it was Aunt Elizabeth's idea to have the girls live with her. Maybe she was just having a bad day and, yet, her comment affected Mom for the rest of her life.

So, Mom might have felt deserted by her well-meaning father, whom she adored, responsible for her younger sister, unwanted by her aunt, abandoned, criticized, and trapped. Her life took a series of terrible turns, first when her mother died when Mom was four, then when she moved from the farm to live with a controlling aunt, and finally when she endured years of an unhappy marriage.

Today Mom's often defensive, overly concerned about what people think of her, and worried about what people think of me since my behavior reflects on her parenting skills.

"Tell me about when you were growing up," I encourage her. Her eyes darken, her voice gets small and far away, "I only want to remember the good times."

She corrects my grammar because her father corrected hers and she says she was grateful for it. She thinks I should be grateful, too. Sometimes she stops me in the middle of telling a story to correct my grammar, and then forgets to ask me to please continue.

"Mom, the story is more important to me than the grammar. I promise that when I send something to a publisher, the grammar will be excellent, and if it isn't perfect, an editor will catch it. That's what editors do."

She purses her lips, disagreeing. She has critical people in her life—Dad, his mom, and society, too, if society were to know about her affair with Janine—so being accurate is very important to her. She can look up the correct grammatical rules and prove to others that she's right—about something, at least.

We're watching the Easter story on TV. Jesus is hanging on the cross, "Father, forgive them, for they do not know what they're doing." Mom speaks to him firmly, "They know not what they do."

You'd think she'd forgive Jesus for the way he worded things. And besides, the English version of what he said on the cross is a translation that theologians and scholars have debated for years.

If I was being crucified (I mean, if I *were* being crucified), good grammar would be the last thing on my mind. I'd be screaming and sobbing and begging for my life; but that's just me. My point is if she corrects "the Son of God" in the last agonizing moments of his life, under those horrific circumstances, there's no hope for me. Can you imagine how hard she is on me, a mere mortal?

Mom exclaims, alarmed, "You said that you send things to publishers. What if they steal it?" Her eyes are wide and anxious.

"That's a chance I have to take, Mom. Someone did plagiarize me in college, but I can't let that stop me from sending my work out. If I never send it out, it'll never be published. Besides, it's rare that publishers steal people's work; if they do it too often, word will get out, no one will send them anything, and they'll be out of business."

She holds on to her fear. "I submitted a greeting card to Hallmark, and someone told me, 'Oh, you'll see it again, but it won't be yours anymore. Hallmark will take your idea, make a couple small changes, create a different card, and not give you any credit.'"

I notice how fret, worry, and distrust stop her from succeeding with her art, and I vow to never again "submit" my work to publishers. Instead, I'll "send" it to them. And they won't "accept" it or "reject" it; they'll either "buy" it or "return" it. Wording it that way will be easier on my ego.

Am I close to Mom? I think I understand her better than anyone in the family, but are we close? I don't know. She said of herself, "The light's on in the attic, but the curtain's pulled" and she flashed a slight, enigmatic smile. She likes that no one can see in; trouble is, she can't see out, either. I'm afraid she'll go to her grave like that, and we'll never have known each other. I grieve that not knowing.

The Mortician's Child

I wish to God that Jesus would come back today. We'd get along fabulously. I have absolutely no fear that he'd condemn me to hell for not believing in original sin or not asking him to intercede on my behalf with God rather than going straight to the Source myself. And besides, if Jesus really *is* God *and* the Holy Ghost (the Holy Trinity), then I'm already there at the Source when I have my "mystical episodes." Of course, I believe that accepting what Jesus said—about loving each other and being non-judgmental—is the way to "salvation," which I interpret as inner peace.

I'll celebrate giving up chocolate by eating another brownie. Like a vaccination, a small bit of chocolate will build up my immunity to it ... *munch* ... that's the theory ... *munch* ... *jeeze*, I'll finish the last one so there aren't any left to tempt me ... *munch* ... *munch* ... *munch* ... there, all gone.

I'm going to remember this bloated feeling if I'm ever tempted to eat chocolate again. *Bleagh!* I mean, I'll *never* eat any more, not because I'm out of it, but just because. Now if I go to someone's house and they offer me a piece of fudge or a brownie, even though I've stopped eating chocolate, I'll have a small piece just to be polite.

26. The Thing Itself

The Thing Itself: the Intelligence from which everything comes, the Power back of Creation — Ernest Holmes

I find my way to a New Thought Science of Mind church (not to be confused with New Age or Scientology). The ministers Jennifer and Jill teach the congregation that people are born good instead of born sinners, which eases the fear that Dad instilled in me that people are basically bad.

They maintain that the universe—visible and invisible—is the mind and body of "God" and we're all individualized expressions of the one "Spirit." Because we're one with It, there's no need to submit to, petition, or bargain with something outside ourselves; all we need do is turn within and recognize the Truth. This is great because I suck at worship; instead, I can simply affirm that what's good and true is mine right now because it's my inherent nature.

Physics validates this unity by proving that the universe is made from the same energy or "Entity," from which we are created, fashioned from the very genetic material of the Universe itself and, therefore, subject to its laws: cause and effect (thought fueled by feelings acting on "Energy" leads to action), attraction (what we think about on a regular basis tends to appear in our lives), circulation (energy is always in motion, life in full, abundant expression), and resurrection (energy is neither created nor destroyed, only transformed).

The congregation holds hands, sings, and sways, "Let there be peace on earth, the peace that was meant to be …. Let there be peace on earth and let it begin with me."

Jennifer and Jill—a couple, it turns out—talk about "the Thing Itself" and why it's important to remember the Source, because from that purity all else evolves. Knowing that we're one with the very essence of the Universe—untouched by words, wounds, and judgments—settles the mind and heart. And so, my goal becomes to live from the awareness of "the thing itself," from the spiritual "unified field" before race, sex, and religion subdivided us.

Dad's way of thinking didn't make him happy. I can choose to think differently. Author Ernest Holmes writes, "Change your thinking, change your life." I'll try this new way of thinking and see what happens. I'll act "as if" it's true.

Jennifer and Jill encourage us to "say positive affirmations," statements of what we want, which help us to "manifest" it in our lives. Mine are "I'm happy, healthy, wealthy, and wise." But they're backed with doubts sometimes: I'm happy (happier than I was in Michigan), healthy (I have low blood sugar and low blood pressure), wealthy (I'm living at poverty level), and wise (I have a way to go). There's a learning curve. Just as challenging is letting people touch me. There's so much indiscriminate hugging in church. I put a smile on my face, "act as if" I like it, and try to learn how to hug.

~~~

I discover one of Grandfather's books in Mom's bookcase, *The Science of Mind*, by Ernest Holmes. It turns out that I'm the granddaughter of Charles Patrick Wade Jones, one of the early New Thought teachers. He taught the philosophy at Joy Farm, later named the "Ministry of the High Watch," meaning to look to the God within.

I knew nothing of my rich, spiritual heritage. I related to him only as a child would to a grandfather whom she visited once in a while. The philosophy that I'd come to love was the one by which he lived for many years. *Science of Mind* magazine published 14 of my articles, which became the basis for my book, *Spirit Incorporated*, dedicated to him. He died before I was published, but maybe he knows—and inspires and guides me in spirit.

27. "Blood and Fire"
Salvation Army Motto

When I graduated from San Francisco State, Jill—the minister from church—who was also a counselor at the San Francisco Salvation Army Harbor Light detoxification center for alcoholics (affectionately referred to as "The Sally"), recommended me for a job as assistant to the Director and General Manager.

Captain Les Sparks, the Program Director, develops and administers policies and procedures, makes sure that standards and regulations are followed, and supervises the programs, but it's the General Manager, Sergeant Major Nick Gabriel, who's aware of the pulse of the place, everywhere at once, all eyes and ears and heart.

I usually finish the office duties early (typing and filing) and have nothing to do so I hang out in the cafeteria and visit with the guys fresh in from detox; or maybe not so "fresh." They drift alone into the cafeteria, pale and shaky, rub their temples, sigh, pour themselves coffee, and light a cigarette.

Here's what happens in the building across the courtyard—behind our building with the offices, classrooms, chapel, and residents' quarters—headaches happen there, sweats, anxiety, depression, seizures, hallucinations, vomiting, diarrhea, and convulsions. Sweat it out, swear it out, get it out. It's a terrible tug of war for the men, the dark addiction on one side, Harbor Light on the other. I wave over whoever wanders in and he comes, tired, hesitant, seemingly thankful that I ask him to join me. I invite their stories.

"I take long coffee breaks," I confess to Nick, as if he hadn't noticed. I hope he'll forgive my slacking off. He's a good-natured, heavy-set guy with a receding hairline. I've never seen him angry. He grins, "That's why you're here, to take long breaks. It's good for the men to practice socializing with an attractive woman while they're sober."

~~~

They appeared in the doorway of my office on my first day, John Fitzgerald and John Cienna from accounting, "Would you like to have coffee with us?" I would *love* to. Imagine that, friends on the first day. Our "battle cry" becomes "*Coffeeee!*"

They become my best friends and confidants. Fitzgerald is Irish, wickedly witty, and keenly observant. He smokes—a lot. Cienna moves slowly, almost sensuously; I feel a tug of attraction. Both came through the detox program, were hired for staff positions eventually, and live in the residents' quarters on the second floor of the office building. Both are fiercely intelligent. They've seen the best and the worst of people. We're laughing over coffee, and they tell me another story, this time about a resident.

Cienna said, "Everyone liked him, and one day he went missing. We figured he started to drink again. It was so depressing. People moped around for days. And then one afternoon, someone came running into the building and said, 'I know where he is! He was hit by a truck. He's in the hospital! People cheered and laughed. *Anything* was better than going back to drinking."

Cienna sips his coffee, tells Fitzgerald and me, "So Nick flew from San Francisco to Los Angeles for a conference, and when he came back he complained about having jet lag."

This is hilarious; we enjoy a good-natured laugh at Nick's expense. San Francisco and L.A. are in the same time zone, of course. That'd be like me getting jet lag on the bus on my way in to work from my apartment in the avenues.

~~~

I like when someone from the detox staff joins me in the cafeteria because I admire them so much. They do the nitty-gritty, front-line work in the trenches: sit with the guys as they go through withdrawal and monitor their symptoms and manage the devastating effects the best they can. Alcohol abuse breaks people down physically, emotionally, socially, and spiritually. Harbor Light shores them up and helps them through in a safe, supportive, spiritually based environment. Sometimes a staff member shares his own experience, "When I was still drinking, I dropped a bottle of vodka in the sink, quickly closed the drain, and strained out the broken glass, so I wouldn't lose a single drop." And this: "When I was five, I sometimes slept in a park because my parents were drinking." That was one of Fitzgerald's experiences; five years old, sleeping in a park, because his parents were crazy drunk.

Verne, also from accounting, joins me in the cafeteria. He's a slim man, in his 50s, who has been sober seven years. He tells me, "When I was still drinking, a friend invited me to his pool party on a Saturday, but I didn't go. I called him on Monday and apologized for missing his party. He said 'What are you talking about? You were here. You ate barbeque ribs, visited with people, and swam in the pool.' I'd had a walking blackout."

"I had one of those," I say, thinking he might be able to give me some insight into my weird brain "episodes." I elaborate, "I was talking with a friend and the next thing I knew I was on the bus going home. I don't remember saying good-bye or getting on the bus." I always wondered what she saw in my eyes while we were talking. Did she have any idea I was unconscious?

"How long have you been sober?" Verne asks.

"Sober? Oh, I don't have a problem with alcohol." *Hmmm*, that's probably what everyone says. "I really don't," I say, more emphatically. "Back in Michigan I got drunk once in college, hated it, and I like to get an occasional buzz on, but two drinks are my limit." Cienna says it takes a lot of booze to get an alcoholic drunk.

"Do you ever hallucinate?" Verne asks.

"Yeah, that happens at night. I saw worms dropping out of the corner of a painting on my bedroom wall, but that stuff happens when I *haven't* had a drink. I moved my bed away from the wall and they dropped onto the floor." Oh damn, that sounds lame. "It's just low blood sugar or low blood pressure."

He nods knowingly and doesn't say anything.

I ramble on, "Actually I suspect that I hallucinate from stress. I think I have post-traumatic stress from when I was a kid."

He sips his coffee thoughtfully.

I stop trying to convince him. I really don't have a problem with alcohol. It's just stress. Dad dropped dead the day that I planned to move here, I have social anxiety, I'm living on $286 a month, and I secretly wonder if Mom is gay. I feel depressed, but now I know that some of my weird "brain episodes" resemble delirium tremors that people experience when going through detox.

And then I realize that I *am* addicted—to a belief in limitation. Here I am working in a detox center, too overqualified—with advanced degrees—to be typing and filing. I like the job, but I need to be challenged mentally and I definitely need to make more money. But I agreed to the duties and the salary and stopped looking for work for which I'm more suited: teaching and writing. This job mirrors my beliefs about prosperity and employment: there are no teaching jobs to be had in this economy and writers starve like Dad said. Every day I see creative, gifted people trade their talents, and their very lives, for their addictions. I've been no different; and yet I blamed the job for my not being professionally challenged or prosperous—the job isn't responsible, I am.

I have an elementary-school teaching degree and a master's degree in reading education. I don't want to teach public school again, or private school, but maybe I could explore another kind of teaching. I know corporate trainers and a friend signed with a speaker's bureau that sends him out on the seminar circuit teaching time management. I'll design a speed-reading-skills seminar and maybe take it "on the road." So, maybe teachers can find work—or create their own courses.

And what do I do day after day at "the Sally"? Write thank-you letters. Maybe I don't say "thank you" enough in my own life. I've focused on what I don't have rather than on what I do: friends, health, an income, and cheerful bosses who let me adjust my schedule if I need time off.

Did Verne notice my "light-bulb" moment? He takes a slow drag on his cigarette.

~~~

Cienna meets me when I come into work, "Verne died last night. He started to drink again."

He was sober seven years! What changed overnight? What if Fitzgerald or Cienna start to drink again and die? I rub my forehead and temples, feeling tired and despondent.

"I didn't know you were close to Verne," Cienna says.

"I wasn't," I sigh. I'm not mourning Verne, although what happened to him is sad, I'm afraid that Cienna or Fitzgerald will disappear—like Dad who died suddenly, and Mom when she ran away from home. Please, Fitz and Cienna, stay sober. I love you.

~~~

We head into the holiday season in fund-raising mode at Harbor Light. Every year the staff and residents prepare Thanksgiving meals to deliver to 2,500 seniors and the disabled. I'm sending invitations to the fund-raising dinner. Cienna and Fitzgerald appear, *"Coffeeee!"*

"I'll be there in a couple minutes, I have to finish these invitations. Should I address Dan White's to Supervisor White or just Mr. White; didn't he resign from the Board of Supervisors?"

The Mortician's Child

"He did," Cienna says, "but he wants back on. Address it to Supervisor Dan White to be on the safe side."

"Okay." I look at the next name on the list of people to invite: Supervisor Harvey Milk, said to be the first openly gay elected politician in the U.S. *Hmmm*, what kind of name is "Milk"?

~~~

I sit next to Dan White at the fund-raising dinner. He's nice-looking and well dressed. I try to engage him in small talk. He's polite, but preoccupied. Is he thinking about the award he'll receive in a few weeks for his police work? Probably not; he's intently watching the Mayor and the Board of Supervisors work the crowd before dinner. His eyes are bright, he has the slight hint of a smile.

~~~

November 27, 1978. Supervisor Dianne Feinstein is visibly shaken on TV: 'Today San Francisco has experienced a double tragedy of immense proportions. As President of the Board of Supervisors, it is my duty to inform you that both Mayor Moscone and Supervisor Harvey Milk have been shot and killed and the .... the suspect is Supervisor Dan White."

http://en.wikipedia.org/wiki/Moscone-Milk_assassinations

Dan White is sentenced to eight years in prison for voluntary manslaughter, a sentence considered too light by many who feel that he deserves the death penalty. It's 8 p.m. A crowd gathers; more than 1,000 people walk from Castro Street toward City Hall. Someone yanks the wrought-iron grillwork off the doors of City Hall and smashes the glass with it; more windows are shattered. A fire is set inside. They're trashing the building.

I watch the news from my apartment in the Avenues. A dozen police cars are torched; sirens wail. The night air is thick with smoke; rioters are silhouettes against the garish lights of vandalized buildings 16 blocks from Harbor Light.

The fury and rage go against my perceptions of gays as marginalized people who don't stand up for their rights. The police drive the crowd from the Civic Center to Market Street where store windows are also broken. People come from all directions to resist the police who receive almost as many injuries as the rioters.

When I was younger, I watched the race riots in Detroit on TV. And now, tonight, after years of being vilified and denigrated, gays riot their despair and anger. I think about Mom's silences. The riots are terrifying, unconscionable; and yet, a part of me wonders sadly, what took them so long?

~~~

I learn years later that the riots in San Francisco were simply the first time that I became aware of the less publicized struggles that LGBTQ communities had been enduring throughout the world. Without the perspective of TV and the Internet, I'd cocooned myself in a narrow life.

28. Making Tracks

*I am invisible … simply because people
refuse to see me.* — Ralph Ellison

    I go to Oakland, from San Francisco, and board the Amtrak train for Michigan. I could have flown but would have arrived too soon. I need time to think and clear my head. After all these years, I need three days more.

    I remember Bill's phone call earlier this week, "I was visiting Mom. She had some women friends over, smoking cigars; Mom had a small pipe. After they left, I asked Mom if she's a lesbian and she said yes." Then, somewhat mystified, it seems, he says, "She has two sons. How does she feel about us?"

    The train lurches and rumbles forward, picks up speed, and carries me toward Mom's revelation, toward what I've been waiting for.

    I packed a few belongings into a small suitcase—warm clothes because it's winter in Michigan—and snacks for the trip. I'm carrying a large, Saran-wrapped, chocolate Bundt cake. I break off a chunk as big as my hand, inhale the chocolate perfume, and bite into it leisurely, intending to make the cake last a long time.

    The train crosses the wide prairies and stops briefly at quaint railway stations along the way to pick up passengers. Two days later I get a migraine, probably from stress. A porter peers into the narrow tunnel of my vision, and asks, "Would you like to see the caboose?" I smile, "No thanks." Actually, I would, but I don't feel like paying what might be the cost of "admission."

~~~

    Why did Mom take so long to come out? I'm just guessing now: because it was her own business, the boys and I might be subjected to public scrutiny, she wanted to wait until we were old enough to understand or wise enough *not* to judge, she figured if we wanted to know, we'd ask?

I visit her once a year. I signed up with a speaker's bureau and now teach speed-reading seminars throughout the country. I quit work at the Salvation Army when the speaker's bureau filled my calendar. One of my clients, the University of Michigan Business School, flies me in once a year to teach a week's worth of workshops to their BA, MBA, and Executive MBA students. After my week there, I visit Mom in Flint, about 60 miles from Ann Arbor.

I go to church with her Sunday mornings, to the strict fundamentalist church where she has good friends—she likes to show me off—and then we socialize later with one of her friends from that church; and sometimes after the first church service, we go to other gatherings attended by members of a Metropolitan Community Church, an all-inclusive Christian denomination that's predominately LGBTQ. I'm pleased that I feel comfortable in both groups. I wonder, though, if it's tiring for Mom to be closeted to one group of friends and out to another. She seems to take it in stride and is well-liked by her friends in both groups.

~~~

Mom lives in a cozy mobile home by a small, pretty lake in Flint, Michigan.

She's living with someone now (a woman with short, fluffy hair that frames her face); Mom and Janine broke up. Mom's new partner went to stay with someone else during my visit, probably to give Mom and me some privacy for our heart-to-heart talk.

"It's so bitter outside," Mom exclaims as she secures the windows against the driving sleet.

I've been here three days and she hasn't come out, yet. The stress is unbearable. And then here it is, "You said once that Dad was concerned about my sexual orientation."

"Yes."

She's silent. She still can't say it.

"Are you gay?"

"Yes."

I start to laugh from the stress. This is where in the movies one person slaps the other to make her stop laughing hysterically and bring her back to the reality of the moment.

"This isn't funny," she says.

I'm still laughing. For some reason it seems funny now, how withdrawn, awkward, alone, and afraid I was growing up, how I got amnesia and maybe had a nervous breakdown and had a sex life that'd make a sailor blush and never told Mom any of it.

"Oh, I know it isn't funny," I agree. I take a deep breath, steady myself, regain my composure, "When did you start to like women?"

"When I was four. I was with my parents and we stopped at a gas station. There was a woman attendant—sort of masculine—and there was something about her that I liked. I told my parents, 'I like that woman.' They took me over to her and had me tell her."

So, Janine didn't "turn her" toward women and Dad didn't turn her away from men. She was born that way. I guess she got married because that was what women did in those days.

It must have been like living in a foreign country where no one spoke her language. She could hear people talking but didn't understand what they were saying; and they wouldn't have understood what she was saying, had she spoken up—and worse, probably would have ostracized her.

My dad didn't like it one bit, of course. Once when I told him that Mom went shopping, he yelled, "She did *not*! She went to Flint to see Janine!"

And Bill told me, "I don't have anything against homos, I just don't approve of their unhealthy, unnatural lifestyle, which leads to

AIDS and pedophilia." He added emphatically, "I'm not anti-gay, I'm pro-normal."

Matt weighs in, saying gently, "I don't think Mom's gay; I think she's just lonely."

I've been so lonely at various times in my life that I was amazed that I didn't die from it and I never, not once, ever thought about "switching teams."

To try to refute my brothers' comments would be pointless—they stand firm on what they believe. That might explain, in part, though, why Mom didn't come out to us before this, for fear of being judged, or never came out at all to her conservative friends.

Mom states, "I had postpartum depression after you were born, but I *never* tried to hurt you!"

"Were you depressed at other times, too?" I'm remembering her crying in the bedroom while Dad was at work, standing by the living room window and whispering (what seemed to be) a prayer into the sunset, and their frequent, heated arguments followed by her silence.

"Oh, yes; I thought about killing myself, but didn't because I had three little children who depended on me."

So, my instincts were chillingly accurate when I was growing up. I was sick with fear that she'd kill herself, but I couldn't imagine how to help her.

"Who was your first?"

"Janine."

"You've been interested in women your whole life and she was your first?"

She nods.

What's it like to be in love, but not able to tell anyone, to find your soul mate in this one precious life that you have, but to be condemned for it, and not allowed to marry?

Mom exclaims, grief edging her voice, "I told Janine that I would have loved her *forever!*"

I don't ask why they broke up, and Mom doesn't offer any details.

She exclaims, "I *really* had it bad for Mrs. Hegel!"

My sixth-grade teacher. That was about the time that Mom started to obsess about the way I looked; to impress Mrs. Hegel any way she could? But Mrs. Hegel was married with children, as Mom was, so even if Mrs. Hegel was so inclined, it wasn't to be.

Mom's mind finds a memory. "When I brought you home from the hospital, you were so quiet; you looked up at me with those big, blue eyes, as if wondering where we go from here?"

Her story fascinates me, as if she handed me a previously missing volume of the encyclopedia full of new definitions, ideas, and facts.

I think about her conservative church; there were two couples who lived together but weren't married. Someone who represented the church told them to either live separately or leave the church. One couple moved into separate houses and the other couple left the church. If living together was that egregious, what would they think of same-sex love?

I ask, "Do they know about you at church?"

"Some people suspect it. One day Reverend Herb came to visit me and said that there was a rumor that I was a homosexual. I told him, 'I don't believe that people can help the way they're born, but I've done nothing wrong.'"

That was the best answer ever. He took it to mean that she hadn't acted on it and was relieved. What she really meant was that she acted on it but didn't consider it wrong.

We continue to talk while we fix dinner. I decide on a stir fry, which takes a lot of preparation: washing, chopping, stirring. It gives me something to do while we talk. "People have no right to tell you who you can love," I say, "like someone thinking that they can give me permission to have blue eyes." That doesn't make any sense, to pick something that people are born with and can't change and make it illegal. I pour myself a glass of white wine that I brought; Mom doesn't want any. She sets the table and I set out the food.

I feel like I'm recovering from a long illness and starting to feel healthy again. I have an expanded feeling, like things are going to be all right. The world is larger, clearer, and full of possibilities.

I lay down my fork, "Since you and Dad were unhappy being married, are you sorry that you had me?"

She seems surprised. "Oh no, I'm so happy to have had you. I love you!" We hug each other and hold on. "Oh, precious, precious," she says, "my precious little girl! I love you so much. You'll never know how much."

~~~

She lights the logs in the fireplace against the cold as the howling wind rages all around us, shaking and rattling the mobile home, looking for a way in. In the island of warmth and light in the storm, we sit in our robes in the kitchen, drink rich cocoa with marshmallows melted on top, listen to the radio playing softly in the background, and discuss the first snow—the way we can sense in advance that it's coming.

The next morning, I pull open the curtains and see crystals, millions of them, softly, silently swirling, flat and sparkling. I bundle up warm and go out to make tracks.

YEARS THAT ANSWERED

THE FOUNDATION
29. Stanchions

Until you make the unconscious conscious, it will direct your life and you will call it fate. — Carl Jung

There's great beauty and depth in the substantial—the spirit within—capable of nourishing and sustaining us.

Many of my thoughts and feelings were an imprint of Mom and Dad's thoughts and feelings—opinions, fears, and frustrations—or a reaction against them. And their thoughts and feelings were an imprint of *their* parents' thoughts and feelings. The "energy" traveled through our family lineage and took on a life of its own until I said "Enough" to what wasn't constructive.

Mom turned to me once when the discord in our family was particularly glaring and exclaimed "What happened to us?" I didn't know what to say; now, having contemplated that for years, I think what happened was because of something that didn't happen, the specter of what could have been; Mom and Dad were grieving their unlived lives where they might have realized their dreams.

My journey will be different. I *will* achieve my goals. I'll be honest and direct with my feelings, learn to communicate clearly, and let intuition guide me. I'll find beauty, grace, and guidance within me, and serenity within my authentic self.

In my dream I'm in the basement of a house (my unconscious mind?) where poles of wood are the reason the whole house hovers, where the Spirit within me is a dry current against the base of stanchions, those supportive, wooden bones. I peel back a thin sliver of wood and discover that music has laid its eggs there.

30. The Physician and the Witch

A house needs two kinds of care: first, maintenance; second, interpretation of its metaphors. For the first, you need a physician, for the second, a witch.

Peter and I met in San Francisco. He was a former NASA rocket scientist and I was a writer—with a newly-earned master's degree—doing office work in a detox center. After a successful career as a rocket designer, Peter decided to work with people instead of aerospace trajectories, and we began to orbit each other.

We moved in together and went into the seminar business—him teaching time management and me teaching speed reading.

Meet Peter the "TimeMan" Turla, and Kathleen Hawkins, "The Speed-Reading Expert."

And then we moved to the Dallas/Fort Worth area, an easy driving distance to the DFW Airport. We each taught 75 to 100 seminars a year throughout the country so living in North Central Texas cut down travel time and jet lag.

And that's how I, a recovering perfectionist, socially anxious, territorial, borderline OCD, wanton writer came to settle down.

I stopped having frightening nighttime experiences, which I now think might have been "hypnagogic imagery," mental phenomena that can occur as one enters a "threshold consciousness" between being awake and falling asleep. This state of mind can include lucid dreaming, such as levitating and out-of-body experiences, and hallucinations like worms dropping out of a picture.

I figure that my hypnagogic experiences were brought on by the stress of making a major life change and a cross-county move right after my dad died. Today my psyche has settled into a gentle hum that's comforting and non-intrusive. It's more my partner now, a friendly companion, rather than a hysterical part of me frantically trying to get my attention. I'm more relaxed now and try to listen to it so it doesn't have to yell.

I'm embarrassed by my earlier hyper-sexuality, but I don't regret it; at the time it distanced me from the death that surrounded me when I was growing up and it made me feel alive. I survived the sexual excursions without catching anything, without negative physical consequences, and I had a great time (looking back through the journal I kept in those days, though, I realize that I frequently felt lost and was trying to find my way socially and emotionally). But now, it's time to stop the risky behavior and calm down. Apparently, it does take a rocket scientist, plus time and introspection.

～～

The old, abandoned house was vacant for three years—before Peter and I moved in—empty except for wasps, spiders, and chimney swallows. Creatures were drawn to it as dreams are attracted to people drifting off to sleep. It was a 3 a.m. kind of house, quiet, eerie, waiting for us.

The house has three levels: on the upper level, a bathroom and the master bedroom; on the second level, two guestrooms, living room, kitchen, more bathrooms; and the lowest level that's built into the hillside where we have a vacant "garden apartment," offices, and a storage area.

My cousin Dawn tells me, "I'm afraid to go into your house." She feeds our cats Simon and Schuster when we travel. I keep their food downstairs on the lowest level. Dawn says, "I tried to get my kid to come downstairs with me, but after the first time, he was too scared to come back to the house, even during the day."

Upstairs, there's a loud *CRACK* like a bullet striking glass, but up by the ceiling. The rocking chair rocks back and forth five times by itself; I huddle on the couch and watch it. This house has phenomena.

~~~

Peter takes care of the maintenance. He's practical, thorough, and patient. He detects and prevents "ailments," like the way things break, wear down, and fall apart. He diagnoses potential flooding problems, scrutinizes cracks in the foundation, cleans the gutters, fixes drainage problems, oversees repairs, and analyzes the direction the wind is blowing in order to scientifically angle the fans indoors for optimum ventilation.

Ever the poet and writer, I look for plot twists. Either things go smoothly, or I have a story. My writer's brain imagines creative causes for the various "phenomena" in the house which increases my sensitivity to more of it.

And I love metaphors. Metaphoric thinking is a holistic approach to viewing the world that gives reality expansion joints, like saying the sun is a lion, or the mind, a computer. Metaphors integrate diverse ways of thinking—science, philosophy, poetry—and are economical; they say a lot with a few words. While science is precise and usually advances humanity, it's just one room of the house of human thought. A house needs all the rooms for people to live in it comfortably.

Rocket designers work with formulas that don't inspire me, like:

> Eccentricity: a Keplerian element describing the shape of the orbit; where: e=0-> circular orbit, e=between 0 and 1->elliptical orbit, e=1->parabolic orbit, e=greater than 1->hyperbolic orbit

I'd rather sit on the deck overlooking the lake and marvel at the moon's nightly orbit and how its light frosts the dark landscape silver and glitters the surface of the water.

~~~

The house has high vaulted ceilings and creaks and groans, shadows and echoes. What adds to the spooky feeling is the fact that it's a big, old house and parts of it are far enough away for a person to not know what's going on in other parts of the house. Subtle energy drifts from room to room, floor to floor.

How like my house I feel, rambling, shadowy, and complex; at once both spacious and cozy. Is my house—in fact, my whole life—largely an out-picturing of my thoughts?

"The house is too choppy," a visitor says uneasily. "When you're downstairs, you're isolated from the rest of the place." That's why I set up my office in a remote room away from distractions. But once when I walked down the hall to my office and passed the door to the empty garden apartment, there was a loud *THUMP* against the other side of the door like something threw itself hard against it to get my attention. I asked a neighbor, "Was there a sonic boom?"

"No."

~~~

At night, I go into the bedroom on the third level, lock the door, and don't come out until morning, especially now when Peter is travelling. I light a candle, step into the bathtub, and disappear in the swirling steam. But tonight, there's a violent thunderstorm spawned by a Category-5 hurricane off the Texas coast. The trees drag their knuckles across the roof, the wind walks chairs across the deck, and there's the clatter of a steady downpour. I forgot to unplug my computer; I leave the safety of the bedroom and make my way downstairs to the lowest level. There's a power outage. The batteries in my flashlight are low; the weak light crosses carpets and feebly stumbles along the floors and across white walls. A small, pale gecko darts into a crack in the corner.

The house isn't cozy or warm. It's drafty and the wooden floors are bare. The cats curl into themselves, paws over their noses.

There's a narrow walkway (with a French drain to keep water from seeping in) behind the wall downstairs. Visitors think they're opening the door to a closet and find themselves in the long, dark passageway. They joke uneasily about not being able to find their way upstairs again.

"Your house overwhelms people," a realtor friend tells me. It sounds almost like a complaint. "And it's really wild out here."

What did he see? Glistening black ravens in the oak trees, a coyote dart across the road, a fox, bobcat, mountain lion? Or has he realized just how far this place is from "civilization," stores, and gas stations. Does it make him feel nervous, vulnerable?

The lights wink on, but one of the bulbs in the lower hall is burned out. The lightning creates an eerie strobe effect, illuminates the hall, darkens it, and illuminates it again.

I forgot to close the drapes on the first floor, in the deepest part of the house. Someone's looking in the window! My heart lurches. A stranded boater who has come up from the lake through the meadow (with its waist-high grass, snakes, and fire ants) at 3 a.m. to ask for help or shelter? He's soaked, hair is plastered to his forehead, face expressionless. He keeps his eyes steady and vacant as if to say, "Look, I'm empty, I'm not a threat."

I blink. He's gone. Looking for a way in? No, not a boater, just a shifting wall of water or maybe my partial reflection. Shaking, I close the curtains.

The ceiling in my office is lower than the ceilings in the rest of the house; it's warmer in here and smells of paper and books. I unplug the computer, leave a light on in the living room, and notice that the chimney leaks; rain trickles down the uneven bricks.

I start back upstairs to the bedroom. There's a sound like a freight train, the ominous voice of a tornado, the walls shudder. I lock the door behind me, turn on a small lamp, and reset the clock. I crawl into the king-sized bed, pull up the thick comforter, and fall asleep. The next morning, the bedroom door—which I closed, locked, and tested—is standing wide open.

~~~

Peter will come home from his business trip, diagnose the storm damage, examine the roof for loose shingles, walk the grounds looking for erosion, and repair whatever broke.

I pick up the scattered lawn furniture and collect the cushions. This morning is cool, fresh, and rain washed, the trees dark and wet. The damp air smells earthy, the grass is greener than yesterday. I sit on the deck, relaxed and peaceful, and let the good sink in.

31. Walk-in Closets

The privilege of a lifetime is to become
who you truly are. — C.G. Jung

There is nothing more beautiful than seeing a person being themselves. Imagine going through your day being unapologetically you. — Steve Maraboli

Sitting in the gay church service in the area where I now live in Texas, I look around at the small group of worshipers and smile, feeling peaceful. I'm probably the only straight person here and I feel totally comfortable. There isn't any homophobia and, even better, not even the possibility of it. I don't have to be on guard for disparaging statements or test people's biases by working progressive comments into casual conversations to gauge their reactions: do they wince, scowl, squirm, frown or, ideally, remain relaxed and open-minded. I don't have to worry about the minister railing against "homosexuals" or congregants quipping, "God loves the sinner, but hates the sin," or "Everyone should be treated with respect, but homosexuality is wrong," or "Being gay should be a private matter between an individual and his God—like alcoholism." Ouch!

> I remember Mom teaching my brothers how to make bread and me to make pies. I didn't have the patience to bake bread: knead the dough, roll it into a ball, dust it with flour, cover with a moist paper towel, wait an hour for it to rise, knead it again and wait some more, knead it another time, and finally bake it. My brothers punched the dough—maybe to work off their excess energy—but I just wanted to mix the flour, vegetable oil, salt, and milk (Mom's recipe), roll it out flat, smooth it into a pie plate, dump in some canned filling, and pop it in the

oven. And I followed her instructions: "Clean up as you go along, put things away, wipe the counters, wash the utensils, clean up after each step in the process, and when you're finished, you'll have a pie and a clean kitchen."

Here in the gay congregation, there won't be any judgmental comments after which I'll need to caution, "Hey, I'm a gay rights advocate," a watered-down version of what I really want to say to a lot of people but can't because I'm in the closet with Mom.

Being with the LGBTQ community, I feel like I've come home to a part of myself because I used to socialize with Mom and her friends; I felt comfortable there, and comfortable here. Much of my life I felt invisible because I belong to a group of people who keep the secret of a gay or lesbian parent still closeted. We're casualties of society's side-stream fear, anger, and misunderstanding. Just as side-stream smoke harms the health of non-smokers, the toxins of homophobia directed at gays harm the families and friends who stand by them, hurt by the negative comments made against them, feeling loyal to them, protective, and keeping the secret; feeling attacked ourselves because we identify with the people we love.

> Before I knew how to write, Mom wrote down the stories I told her, and read them back to me. And when I learned to write, she gave me pads of paper for birthdays, Christmas, and Easter so I could write down my stories and, by doing so, she instilled in me a love of reading and writing. And she saved the stories; I can read them now, as an adult, and appreciate the creative little soul I was.

> And when they taught me as a child in Sunday school to pray, "Now I lay me down to sleep, I pray the Lord my soul to keep; if I should die before I wake, I pray the Lord my soul to take," she said, "Say it this way instead, 'Now I lay me down to sleep, I pray the Lord my soul to keep. Guide me through the starry night and wake me with the morning light.'"

When I grew up in the conservative Midwest in the 50s and 60s, I didn't know any kids at school whose parents were divorced, let alone having a same-sex affair. Men loving men was illegal in the United States (women weren't on the radar in those days), and it was a crime in the rest of the world, too. And so, Mom was "in the closet." Had she been out—she, who loved, taught, fed, and rescued me—she would have been targeted for discrimination, condemnation, and legislation against her. So, we kept the secret.

> When I was little, Mom assured and rescued me. When I got stuck in the muddy backyard, she saved me; I marveled at how she could walk on mud when I was sinking in what I knew was quicksand.

> When I climbed a tree in the yard and was too terrified of heights to come down, she climbed up after me and guided me safely back to the ground, "Step down with your right foot, there's a branch there, good, now step down with your left foot, hold on with both hands, another branch on your right, good, you're almost there, I've got you, I'm here …"

> And when I was sure that there was a bear outside the tent on a family camping trip—sniffing, snuffling, and snorting right outside—she risked her own safety to go

> investigate, and reported back to me, "It's just the man in the next tent snoring."

When I was 16, I wondered if there were a chance that I might be gay, too. It's a misconception that children of gay parents have a greater "risk" of being gay themselves, when in fact, they have about the same chance as children of straight parents. Turns out I was turned on by boys with an intensity that stunned me and a passion that lasted, but I didn't ask Mom's dating advice; I was afraid she wouldn't understand. Even though she dated and married my dad, her experiences would have been vastly different from mine since her true orientation was deemed a sin and a crime. A woman was expected to get married and raise a family, and so she did.

I felt lonely and isolated. Had Mom felt free to live openly, I doubt that she would have married; if that meant I wouldn't have been born, well, okay. I love my life, but if I'd never been born, I couldn't have missed something that I didn't have in the first place.

> When I was in junior high school some kid designated Thursdays as "Queers' Day," and told everyone to wear pink and talk with a lisp. I didn't know any gay kids. I half-heartedly rummaged through my closet for something pink—go along to get along—but I didn't have anything pink and didn't look good in the color, anyway; besides, I thought the idea was stupid and depressing. When I told Mom about it being Queers' Day, she said, "Don't spread that information."

The last time I visited Mom, I asked, "Why do you go to such a strict church? Why not go to a 'welcoming' church, like a Unitarian Universalist church or a Metropolitan Community Church?"

She answered, speaking of Reverend Herb at her church, "I don't always agree with everything he says, but he's such a good speaker."

She has two sets of friends, one group from the fundamentalist church, and the other group, lesbians. At the first church, she volunteers at roast-beef fundraisers, visits shut-ins, and was a deacon. They don't know her secret, but my father, brothers, and I knew; her closet became a walk-in closet, and we were all in there together. That's the way secrets work.

So being in the closet with Mom, I've been "treated" for years to negative comments that gays and lesbians endure often and directly. Whenever I visit Mom, she takes me to her fundamentalist church and proudly shows me off. Once during "coffee and donuts" after the service, a man asked with a smile and a twinkle in his eyes, "So what do you think of all those fruits and nuts in San Francisco?" He probably assumed that I felt the same way he did. I shrugged, "It doesn't bother me." He looked astonished and a little perplexed and irritated; my response didn't compute (shouldn't everyone disapprove of, and joke about, "those people"?). My mom—whom he considers a friend—was sitting next to him, talking with someone else and apparently didn't hear what he said.

When I introduced Mom to my neighbors here in Texas when she was visiting from Michigan I didn't say, "Mom, these are my neighbors, they're straight," so I certainly didn't say, "Neighbors, this is my mom, she's a lesbian." A person's sexuality shouldn't figure into an introduction. So now they know someone who's a lesbian—but they don't know it—and they like her. I hope they don't think I was trying to trick them by not telling them, to prove to them that they can like someone who's a lesbian; I just couldn't determine a proper segue in our conversations, and I'm afraid they'd turn away from me (we've been friends for years). Such are the thoughts that run through my mind and consume valuable time and energy.

~~~

After the gay church service, I march in a parade for equal rights. I'm wearing rainbow wristbands. I go to the parade to be counted and walk in support of Mom who's 84 years old now and too frail to attend a parade, but she wouldn't march anyway. She'd be asked to leave the church she loves if the truth came out.

A newspaper article written later about the march reported "These events are getting bigger every year, attended by increasing numbers of gays and lesbians." There was no mention of the growing numbers of allies, friends, and families who march proudly alongside them.

I do an Internet search for "children of gay parents" and 139,000 results pop up. I discover books and interviews, organizations, and associations. I learn that there are between six and 14 million children with gay parents, numbers that can only be estimated because so many parents are still in the closet.

I read voraciously until I feel woozy with all the new information. In the heart-wrenching book, *Prayers for Bobby*, a mother comes to terms with the suicide of her son. Prior to his death, she couldn't accept him being gay. Although she loved him dearly, she was disappointed in him, lectured him relentlessly against being gay—often quoting the Bible—and incessantly tried to change him. He jumped to his death off a highway overpass. Today she's a gay rights activist.

I read *Families like Mine: Children of Gay Parents Tell it like it Is* and laughed with relief and cried because I relate, and I started to breathe again; I wasn't the only kid with a gay parent, I never was, there are so many others.

I also read *The Mayor of Castro Street*, about Harvey Milk. It chills me every time I remember that I sat next to Dan White at a Salvation Army Harbor Light fundraising dinner a couple weeks before he assassinated the Mayor and Harvey Milk.

After the assassination, people speculated about White's motives, one theory being that he'd resigned from the Board of Supervisors but asked to be reinstated. The Mayor said "No" and Harvey Milk supported the Mayor's decision. So, White was probably angry about that. And he was on record for making anti-gay comments and was the only supervisor to vote against an ordinance that prohibited employment discrimination against gays.

In those days I was an impressionable young college student with a lesbian mom, so whatever White's motive, it was a cautionary tale for me that sometimes there are assassins in our midst, we don't know what's going on in other people's minds, and we'd be wise to be careful with whom we share our secrets.

~~~

Mom's friends are frantic on the phone, "We dropped your mom off last night after church and when we came back today to pick her up for lunch, the chain lock was on the door, but the door was open. She didn't answer the door, so we called Reverend Herb. He came and broke it down. She's been lying on the bathroom floor for about 18 hours!"

A sinking feeling of dread spirals me back to when Dad died suddenly. Mom, you can't die; I'm not ready to lose you.

"We tried to lift her, but we're not strong enough. She says she doesn't want an ambulance, but we called one anyway."

I sit and stare while Peter books a flight for me to Michigan. Weather forecast: 20 degrees below zero with heavy snow. Mom, you came out to me during a winter storm; please don't die in one.

~~~

Her friend Barb meets me at the airport and takes me to Mom's place where I find her car key and drive to the hospital.

Apparently, she tripped in the living room, pitched forward, and hit her forehead on the corner of the wall. Then (just speculating now), ever concerned with appearances, she was afraid that someone would look in the living room window and see her on the floor so she crawled down the hall to the bathroom—instead of to the phone for help—and lay there on the floor until her friends found her.

She smiles when I come into the hospital room but doesn't seem surprised to see me. She looks frail in the bed, her skin translucent, her hair wild and white like a dandelion gone to seed.

～～

When I was growing up, I found solace in the circle of her arms, a circle that enlarged to accommodate me as I grew, just as my arms cushion her when I bring her home from the two-week hospital stay.

I fix us dinner and clean up after each step in the process as she taught me to do. Now we're sitting in the living room and I say gently, "Mom, when you fell you were on the floor for 18 hours."

She counters with, "Oh no, I don't think it was that long."

"It was about 18 hours from the time Barb dropped you off that night and came to pick you up for lunch the next day, and the doctor said that it was that long judging by the rate at which your organs were shutting down. You had a very serious fall."

"Oh, I could have gotten up."

"But you didn't, and you were in the hospital for two weeks."

"Was it that long?"

I want to impress upon her how serious it'd been so she'll be more careful and won't fall again, as if realizing that she almost died would be all it'd take to keep her safe in the future. "The doctor said we almost lost you. You almost died."

"I did?"

She continues to minimize the seriousness of the fall. "Well, the woman in the bed next to me fell off a ladder and broke her neck. That's much worse than what happened to me."

I think fiercely, but she's not *mine. You're* mine.

I'm sitting on the couch. She falls asleep in the big chair by the TV. I think about all that we've been through and shared as I was growing up and she was growing toward her more authentic self. We were both looking for validation and love. And I realize how people are more similar than different. After all, what's the "gay way" to read a story to your baby, grocery shop, teach your children to bake, or drop your kids off at school? What's the "gay way" to save your daughter from a tree too tall, quicksand, imaginary bears, or a frightening children's prayer that suggests that she might die during the night?

As the shadows outside lengthen across the snow and evening deepens, I watch her sleep and I whisper, "I pray the Lord our souls to keep, guide us through the starry night and wake us with the morning light."

THE MYSTERY OF LOSS

32. "What a Party Line!"

The cure for anything is saltwater—
sweat, tears, or the sea. — Isak Dinesen

Father Paul Keenan of the Archdiocese of New York and I met when four of us authors were working with an Oprah producer to put together a show on spirituality in business (my first brush with Oprah was when a producer wanted to feature my book *Spirit Incorporated* on the show, but Oprah discontinued her "Remembering Your Spirit" segment and started her own network.

Paul and I became friends and shared many heartfelt emails. He was a host at WABC: Religion on the Line and WOR: As You Think. He interviewed me about *Spirit Incorporated* on "As You Think." He told me, "People tell me they don't know how I do radio; television, they say, is so much more connected—radio seems like talking to nobody. They don't realize that's the point. I'm talking into that void, that zone. And in doing that, I'm talking to myself, to God, and to everybody, all at the same time. What a party-line!"

When Paul lost his best friend on 9/11 in the World Trade Center attack, he emailed me: "How is it that the mystery of loss works to give us life when all we feel is loss?"

I had plenty of opportunity to think about death growing up the child of a mortician and losing Dad when I was in my early 20s. I answered: "Maybe loss makes us feel more alive because grief is fierce and immediate. It forces us to pay attention and makes us aware that we need to belong to someone, to the world, and to something greater than we are. Loss makes us participants in the drama and mystery of Life. It gives us a common bond and an opportunity to rise above the pain and make something of it. When we feel loss, we can turn to a higher, greater, deeper power than ourselves and feel that comforting, necessary connection. We belong to Life and belong to each other."

He emailed back: "How is it that two people who don't communicate very often actually never for a moment lose touch? Your answer is brilliant, a wonderful gift to me. I love the many dimensions to it. I'm so grateful for it. You said things that I was having trouble conceptualizing and saying."

～～～

We got busy with our respective projects and things got quiet. I went online to see what he was up to before I emailed him and discovered that he'd had a heart attack and died three days before his birthday. I was stunned and found some comfort in what he'd emailed earlier: "How is it that two people who don't communicate very often actually never for a moment lose touch?"

Just as we have physical bodies made of systems that depend on each other—circulatory, respiratory, digestive, muscular, and a skeletal system that holds it all together—we have "energetic," emotional bodies made of interrelated feelings, experiences, and relationships, and a "spiritual essence" that transcends individual consciousness and holds it all together. Maybe there's no separation of emotional bodies. The "spiritual" is as real as the physical and, perhaps, survives it. Maybe we never lose touch with each other even if death seems to separate us. "What a party line!"

A party line, for my younger readers, many of whom just use smartphones (LOL), was a telephone landline shared by multiple subscribers. They could pick up the phone and hear their neighbors talking. Maybe the Universe still has humanity on a party-line.

As it turns out, Death has a few more sad surprises for me: the loss of a niece and nephew born too soon, my 14-year old cat Schuster, and my mother.

33. Jack
Listen to life, and you will hear the voice of life
crying, "Be!" — James Dillet Freeman

He's about four years old, running wildly through the airline terminal. His mom—busy with a baby, and juggling carry-on luggage, diaper bag, and other paraphernalia—tries to corral him with her voice, "Jack, come here. Get over here now."

They board early so they're already seated when I get on, Jack is in his own seat next to his mom. He's screaming, "I want out of here!" He shrieks and wails, over and over, "I want out of here! I want out of here!" He's hysterical and doesn't notice my disapproving scowl. He's tiny sitting in the oversized seat, seatbelt fastened securely across his lap holding him prisoner, tears streaming down chubby little cheeks. His screaming sets off his baby sister, too, and now they're both screaming—in stereo. A passenger exclaims, "I think I've died and gone to hell."

"I want out of here!" Jack screams.

I think, "Yeah, Jack, I want you out of here, too."

His mother is surprisingly patient, "Jack, once the plane takes off you can sit in my lap and look out the window." That doesn't pacify him; he's still screaming. This is a three-hour flight. I won't be able to stand him for that long.

And then I remember something my brother Matt said about his babies, my niece and nephew. Due to problems with the pregnancy, they were delivered three months prematurely and placed in incubators. "They have more tubes going in and out of them than a cheap TV set," he muses, trying for a little bit of levity in a dire situation. In addition to all the hospital equipment that's monitoring the babies and helping to keep them alive, there are feeding tubes going into their noses, down their throats, and into their stomachs.

He and my sister-in-law, who live in South Africa at this writing, see them every day. He says that the only sounds in the ICU are the hospital machines, voices of the medical staff whispering, and parents crying.

My nephew lived a week. Matt picked up the birth certificate and death certificate on the same day. My niece lived 21 days. Matt said sadly, "I never heard them cry."

The feeding tubes made it impossible for them to express their pain, fear, or confusion. And Matt never heard his children's voices before they died. "I never heard them cry."

My thoughts turn to Jack who is still crying. Yeah, he's annoying, but when I think about Matt's babies, silent until the end, unable to cry, Jack's protests don't seem as bad anymore. Jack's mom pulls him onto her lap, fastens her seatbelt around the two of them, and he calms down. All I hear is the drone of the engines.

Now when I hear children crying in a store, on a plane, or in some other public place, it doesn't bother me anymore because I remember two babies who never cried, who couldn't cry, and how we wished they could.

34. Schuster
God made the cat so we might have the pleasure of caressing the tiger. — Author Unknown

I stand in the living room and call, "Schuster, Schuster," just to hear the familiar sound of my voice saying his name, expecting him to run out from a bedroom, or run up from downstairs, and answer me with purrs or inquiries about dinner. All I hear are echoes. I gave him permission to haunt me, so I expect him to come.

I said my "final" good-bye after the vet told me in May that Schuster had three or four days to live, then I said my final good-bye before a business trip to Michigan in September, and then again before a trip to northern California. I told him each time to do what he needed to do when the time was right and die peacefully at home knowing that he was dearly loved. I assured him I'd understand.

Fluid had built up around his lungs and compressed them to half their capacity, his breathing rapid and labored. The veterinarian ordered lab work and drained him like a radiator, but, despite that, Schuster continued to be a cheerful little fellow with very big purrs in him.

I think it was a fall. He used to sit on a ledge over a stairwell by the bedroom door and wait for me to get up in the morning. If he'd fallen off the ledge, it would have been about a 10-foot drop onto the stairs below. That could have caused a sharp blow to the chest. I used to scoop him off the ledge, hug him close to me, and carry him downstairs. "Elevator going down," I'd say, and scold gently, "Be careful you don't fall when you sit up there," and he purred like it was a game.

I agonize about Schuster's failing health in emails to a friend, Pat, and she replies, "I think there comes a time when the kindest thing we can do for our loyal and loving companions is to be sure that suffering occurs only when there is hope."

I'm grateful he lived five months longer than the vet said he would, and he left on his own, according to his soul's timetable. I was on a trip. Peter was home. He told me that "Schuster spent his last day curled up purring on my lap in the office and sat on my desk and watched me work. His spirits were good. I went upstairs for a snack, came back, and found him lying on the floor by the desk."

~~~

Schuster is in the meadow now, just beyond the backyard, not too far from Simon, and presiding over rabbits, birds, field mice, and the changing of the seasons, and there will be wildflowers in the spring.

I walk casually now instead of with the careful, measured steps of one who expects a cat to appear underfoot. And when I feel lonely, I think, please, come back and haunt me, please.

I walk back and forth from the house to his grave to show him the way home and I whisper, "It's this way, sweet spirit. Follow me."

35. Wounded

This is a wound, a terrible injury,
losing, leaving, letting go.

This is my last time to:

- Sleep in Mom's cozy guest bedroom, visit with her friends, and walk by the peaceful, beautiful lake that she loved
- Eat at her favorite restaurants in her honor: The Old Country Buffet, the Grand Traverse Pie Company, and the Bavarian Inn in Frankenmuth, Michigan
- Sit in "her" pew at church, the seat she came early every Sunday to claim (and once went on a Saturday by mistake); today the choir sings, "Just a Closer Walk with Thee"

Amid the memories and all the familiar places, only the funeral home is new, a 50,000-square-foot facility with thick carpets and 18 sparkling chapels; she lies in one of them wearing a deep burgundy blazer with a delicate, tri-color flower brooch (red, rose, and wine), a crisp white, tailored shirt, and a rose scarf at her neck. The funeral director put the items we gave him in the casket with her: a lovely note from her granddaughter, pictures of her sister and father and a stuffed dog, Tara, which Mom named after a dog she loved who died a few years before her.

My brothers and I hold hands and approach the casket with our love, guilt, and good-byes; both parents, dead of heart attacks, 39 years apart.

Because Dad was a mortician, it wasn't strange to ask Mom, on one of my many visits, about final arrangements or what song she wanted sung at her funeral. She said, "How Great Thou Art." We're not having a funeral for her, just a visitation, so I printed out several copies of the lyrics. Matt closes the chapel doors before people start to arrive for the visitation, and he and Barb and I stand by the casket and try to sing it. All three of us are good singers individually, but he doesn't know the music, so he makes up something, Barb sings harmony because that's what she sings in the choir, and I can't sing the melody by myself if I don't have anyone to follow. My nephew Greg (Bill's son) video records our substandard endeavor; the sound doesn't turn out—probably a good thing—but I'm sure that our efforts would have amused Mom.

We remove the pictures and leave the note and stuffed dog with her. The next day we pick up her ashes from the funeral home and, after a private ceremony that evening in her small kitchen, just my brothers and I sharing memories and reading poetry, we take her to a spot that she loved: a "fairy ring" circle of mushrooms poking up from the grass and bordered by beautiful trees, and let the wind carry her ashes away in the moonlight.

Grief is strangling me—I can hardly breathe. I look through her things quickly because I have a flight home in a few days. I go through dresser drawers, closets, and cupboards, decide what to keep, donate, recycle. In the guest bedroom, I slide back the closet door and there on the upper shelf are journals, eight of them. I gather them to my chest; I can't believe my good luck! What a treasure, windows into her soul. I pack them in my carry-on luggage to read when I get home.

At home, I curl into a ball in bed, pull the covers over my head, and pass out from exhaustion. I'd researched independent senior retirement homes for Mom in California (where my brother Bill lived), Michigan (where she lived), and Texas (where I lived), unsure where she'd end up. As she began to slip physically and mentally, I researched the next level of care—assisted-living facilities in the three states, and then nursing homes and hospice services—and Matt researched travel plans to come from overseas where he lived to see her and ask her what she wanted to do.

When she was alive, I agonized out loud to myself, "Where's the best place for her?" and I heard a startling answer from out of nowhere, *I wanted her two years ago.* That was when she fell and lay on the floor for 18 hours. Was she meant to die then; but how could we *not* have done everything possible to save her life?

A couple of people told me at the visitation that Mom said she didn't want to move, didn't want to leave her place by the pretty lake where she lived for almost 40 years. So, in the end, she got to stay.

Bill told me, "When Mom and I were out running errands and she waited in the car, I'd tell her, 'Don't talk to anyone except me and Jesus,' and she'd say gently, 'Jesus is already here.'"

I found the following quote by Rabindranath Tagore in her things, written in her handwriting: "Death is not extinguishing the light; it is only putting out the lamp because the dawn has come."

~~~

I think about my family and friends still here and, at night in bed when Peter falls asleep before I do, I listen with wonder and reverence to the music of his breathing.

REDEMPTION

36. The Journals

If you read somebody's diary, you get what you deserve. — David Sedaris

Top row: Mom's journals. Bottom two rows: my diaries and journals, which I started to keep when I was 13.

Several months after Mom's death, I'm ready to read the journals that she kept in high school, college, and the early months of her marriage; ready to read her inner thoughts and feelings.

I pour myself a glass of Riesling and turn to the first page in the first journal. She writes:

> It's going to be a great comfort keeping a journal because there are so many things I think that I can't tell anyone. Of course, I won't be able to put them all down in writing for that would take volumes, but it'll be nice when I'm feeling blue to open my journal and write, and when I'm feeling happy, too.

I'm surprised and amused to discover that she was quite a prankster, although I personally don't like practical jokes:

- When Mom was a schoolgirl, the girl sitting in front of her was wearing a dress with a sash, which Mom tied to the girl's chair so when the girl was called on to go to the chalkboard, she was stopped short.
- Mom also planned to rig a bucket of water above a doorway in the church recreation room so when the kids came in for a "Young People's Social," the bucket would tip over and spill water on them; she sketched out the plans in her journal. But her dad mentioned that he was going to the church early to make sure that things were ready for the social, so Mom changed her plans and "I made cotton-filled cream puffs instead."
- She hid her bowl of ice cream under the table so the servers at the social would think that she hadn't received any and give her some more.

Mom was confident, observant, and playful at an early age. I miss her so much. The world is lonelier without her in it.

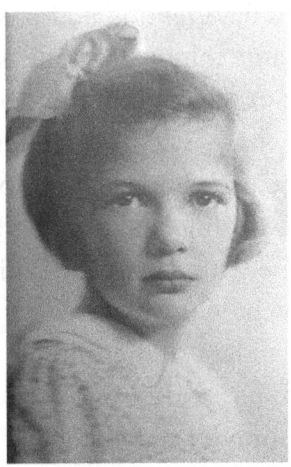

I spent much of my life trying to understand her, but she was guarded and private, and when she finally "came out" to me as we sat in her cozy, warm kitchen while a winter storm raged outside, I thought she answered my questions. Now reading her journal, it seems that she did have a few boyfriends. I suppose that was the "proper" thing to do in those days if you were a girl and then a woman—have boyfriends and, eventually, a husband—even if you were attracted to the same sex. But Mom didn't have sex with any of her boyfriends. Dad told me that he and Mom were both virgins when they got married.

Then he added, sadly it seemed, speaking of me, "I think that *you* were a virgin until your first boyfriend in college." He said it like he was asking a question, like I'd tell him something personal like that! What a creepy, inappropriate conversation that would be. I think that my silence confirmed his suspicions.

Mom told me that she had doubts about marrying Dad a week before the wedding, but figured it was just nerves.

~~~

I continue to read Mom's journals. How much like me she was, full of longing and hope; I feel like I'm reading my own writing and talking to myself. It's disorienting and unsettling. She writes, "No two people see the same things the same way."

True in the case of me and my brothers—three years and seven years younger than I am—who try to tell me how it was for us growing up. We were each born into our parents' marriage at different stages of its decline and each had our own unique, interpersonal dynamic with Mom and Dad and each other.

They can't know how it was for me by using their own experiences as the standard of measurement, any more than I can tell Bill that I know what he went through in Vietnam because I read a couple books, saw a movie, and watched coverage on the nightly news. I *can't* speak for him. Nothing equals having been there—inside his own skin. I won't deny my brothers their perception of their own experiences. I'll let them write their own stories.

~~~

Mom wanted to be a missionary, travel the world doing good, and then fade into the background and not take any credit for her good works. Another time she wanted to be a ghost:

> Wouldn't it be fun to be a ghost? I'd be born on October 31; ghosts can choose their date of birth, can't they? But I'd never touch a broomstick. Instead I'd ride on the wind and sprinkle stardust on hayfever victims.

I fill my glass a second time; it's a mistake. I start to cry. As I read Mom's journals, I feel omnipotent, like I'm a parent watching a child that I love walk slowly toward a busy highway and I know she's going to get hit, but I'm helpless to do anything about it. I want to stop her, to shout, "Major in art instead of music in college (even though you're a talented vocalist, you'll wish you made other choices), don't marry Dad (you'll be unhappy), eat heart-healthy foods (a heart attack will claim you).

~~~

She writes in pale, green ink:

> I can see some grandchild reading through my journals with an expression of bewilderment on his or her face, then when he or she is through, an exclamation, "What a strange girl my grandmother must have been!" It would be nice if they could understand. But perhaps you're not a grandchild; you're a niece, nephew, or cousin.

How about a daughter? Could she not have predicted me? She continues:

> Perhaps you're my father or sister, a friend, or perhaps no relation, but whoever you are, can you understand? Many of my problems are yours, some are different, but I'm trying to record my thoughts as they come, and if it's a bad job, who's to lose—not I, for I've enjoyed it. No, if it's a bad job, you're the one to be dissatisfied for spending the time reading it; and if by any slim chance, it has helped—I'm glad.

Mom, it's helping more than you can know, helping me to keep you a little longer and hold you a little closer, to see you as you were growing up, and to know you a little better.

Reading her journals throws me into an altered state: I look into her past (in which I didn't exist) from the present (in which she doesn't exist), and I know her future (how and when she's going to die), and this awareness is all happening in the moment; past, present, future, superimposed, and all tangled up.

This has been a year of firsts without her: Mother's Day, my birthday (ironically on Mother's Day), her birthday, Halloween (her favorite time of year), Thanksgiving, and now, Christmas. I want to scold her, "Just stop it and be here, quit hiding," like she's watching me from a great distance, but can't speak, like she can choose to do something other than be dead.

I whisper, "I can't speak to you, either, because I'm from the future you never lived to see."

She writes—wise beyond her years—something in which I take comfort:

> They played a piece called "Elegy." It was melancholy, but strangely sweet. It started out so sad and slow, and then

sounded glad and victorious at the end. Maybe that's the way it is when you die—sad when you leave your friends and loved ones, but when you stop looking back, and look forward instead, your soul exalts because of its glorious freedom.

I remember Mom's stubborn, unwavering independent nature—how hard it must have been for her to feel trapped in an unhappy marriage—maybe as hard as it was for me to feel trapped growing up in an unhappy family with a depressed father—with a grim job—who was volatile, critical, and unpredictable.

Then I moved to San Francisco to live on my own, make new friends, and get on with my life, and Mom divorced Dad to live on her own, make new friends, and get on with her life. She bought a cozy, two-bedroom home by a pretty lake. She told me that when she first moved there, she went skinny-dipping one night. She was such a wild child.

~~~

I start to read the next journal. She seems to have had mystical experiences, too. I remember her saying, "One day you feel close to God. It doesn't happen to everyone." She writes about her "spells," when she wants to become a vagabond and hop aboard a passing freight train and take off into the world for parts unknown; the beauty of nature, a distant train whistle, and a tingling in her solar plexus sets it off. I've felt similar tingling, too, like something trying to alert me to the fact that I could expect a creative day ahead working on my writing, and most recently, as I lay in bed mourning her loss, I felt an external "tapping" up and down my solar plexus, "someone" playing me like a keyboard; maybe Mom trying to get my attention, "I'm here, I'm here, I'm here."

Were her "spells" my "mystical episodes"?

She mentions singing a solo in church, "In the Garden." I find the hymn on YouTube and sing along because people say that I sound like Mom did.

~~~

Her very last journal entry was about her unrequited love for someone who smiled at her and walked away. She wrote it before she met Janine, so I think that it was Mrs. Hegel, my sixth-grade teacher.

Then the journal stops, midway through, the rest of the pages torn out. I turned to that last day in *my* diary, the same date and year; I was 15. I wrote that Mom was unhappy, but wouldn't tell me why, and that she took off her wedding ring never to wear it again.

It was eerie to read what we each wrote about that last day. Sometime later Mom met Janine, also married with children, and I guess they fell in love; Mom told Janine that she would love her forever. But that didn't work out, either. Mom had other same-sex relationships, and then one of the women moved in with her. They lived together for several years until she moved away to be closer to her mother who was having health issues.

Whatever the circumstances of Mom's relationships, I truly hope that she had enough happiness in her life to outweigh the bad.

The smoke alarm is going off upstairs; time to replace the battery?

~~~

I pick up one of the journals to reread an entry; it's what I was looking for: there's a "secret" that her friend—a girl—confides in her, which Mom says that she dares not put in writing. She alludes to "the secret" a couple times, and to: "… strange thoughts I can't begin to tell anyone, thoughts sometimes smiling, beckoning and so wistfully beautiful, and other times dark and painful."

She mentioned her friend's name. I look her up on the Internet and find her marriage announcement. When both women grew up, they married men, the thing to do according to society's standards at the time. People would have considered Mom and her friend's attraction—if they did love each other—an affliction, a crime, and a sin.

But I'm so relieved to know that Mom seems to be at peace with, what I assume, was their mutual attraction when they were teenagers. She and her friend sleep in the hayloft. One day they collect the letters that they wrote to each other, set them on fire, and throw them into the river. Mom writes in her journal: "I feel so peaceful now—it's hard to explain. But I do know it's as if God were smiling at me and I was able to smile back without a guilty conscience. It's a wonderful feeling."

Mom wrote in the hayloft, too, and had to climb a ladder to get up there:

> The semi-circle on the red binding of my journal was made by my lips. I have only two hands and the hayloft is an excellent place for writing. My hands were busily occupied in getting me up there and consequently I put my book between my teeth and ascended that way.

I close the journal, examine the red binding under a lamp, and see the faint imprint of an upper lip: Mom's, when she was 17. I press it to my cheek.

37. The Gift of the Speed Bump
Victims are angry people. — Byron Katie

It was one of those bad days; nothing was going right—meaning things weren't going exactly the way I wanted them to. I had my errands mapped out; making mostly right turns all day long. I was going to the bank first and then the grocery store, lunch, blood donation center, office supply store, and hair salon. Well, one place opened later than I expected—and I was hungry—the blood donation center was closed, the grocery store didn't have the item I wanted, and before I knew it, my perfect plan wasn't perfect any more, and I had to make left turns, which made me anxious. I put up with crap when I was a kid, Dad yelling and my brothers teasing me relentlessly (Bill admitted he tried to "get my goat" because it could so easily be gotten). And I didn't have any control over Mom and Dad dropping dead without any warning, but now that I'm an adult, I won't take grief from anyone or anything!

As I drove through a store parking lot, there it was up ahead, a speed bump so huge that I had to slow way down and ease my way up and over it. And there were other speed bumps beyond that, mocking me, all arranged so I couldn't go around them, I had to go over them. And even though I didn't intend to speed, the speed bump inconvenienced me. I yelled and swore at it and, suddenly, it was as if I stepped outside myself, and was watching myself: alone in a parking lot yelling at a speed bump. It was silly. Did I think that a road crew was going to come along, apologize for putting it there, take out their jackhammers and remove it—because I was upset? I was angry out of proportion to what was going on.

That was the day I realized the difference between non-productive anger—being furious at something I can't do anything about, like the speed bump—and productive anger, being angry at something I can do something about, and then acting constructively, like participating in a good cause or making a change for the better.

I remembered Dad's anger, most of which didn't seem productive. Yelling made him look out of control, powerless, and like a victim and made me go silent around him. And then I had an eerie feeling that it was *him* yelling *through* me at the speed bump. I got the chills. I must have internalized his belief that people—and things—frustrate, disappoint, and confound us.

Did anger make us feel more alive by being able to feel so strongly about something? It seemed to energize Dad and, when I was growing up, my anger kept imagined danger at a distance and fueled my creativity. Sometimes I felt relieved to feel angry and depressed because that was better than feeling nothing; a step up from apathy.

A lot of people seem angry these days because they're being robbed of their peace of mind—slowly, on the installment plan—speed bump by speed bump, clerk by clerk, jerk by jerk. Oh wait, correction: they let themselves be robbed by not dealing with their anger constructively. It's not the speed bumps that are our undoing, it's the things we say to ourselves about them that eat away at us and erode our health, happiness, and well-being.

Now when I feel angry, I ask if there's something constructive I can do; if yes, I do it; if no, I try to remain calm and clear-headed.

As it turns out, it was a perfect day, speed bump and all, because I learned a valuable lesson: the difference between the two angers, productive and non-productive. I also realized the extent to which I internalized my father's negative beliefs. And I began to relax my need to be right all the time and to have others behave exactly the way I want them to.

38. Hush Little Baby, Don't You Cry, I'll Sing You a Lullaby

A mystical symphony permeates my senses and a
holy lullaby embraces me. — Earthschool Harmony

There was a tug of war for you with your mom on one side telling you one thing, "You *could* be so pretty if you'd just do something with your hair and wear a little makeup," and the world on the other side telling you another, that you were very pretty; and your dad suggesting that you were stupid and the world presenting you with awards, scholarships, and advanced degrees. You were hurt, confused, and angry.

Hush, little baby, don't you cry, I'll sing you a lullaby. I curl up and wrap my arms around myself, pull you to me, my precious inner child. I apologize for hurtful things I've said to you and for the fear I felt. Now I honor and respect you. I carry your picture—myself as a little girl—in my wallet so if I catch myself backsliding and criticizing you, I look at it and apologize, "I'll do better, I promise. I'll be kind to you. I'll earn your trust."

~~~

When you were a child you related to the world as a child with no frame of reference. Every experience was new. You fell and skinned your knee and it was terribly upsetting. The next time you fell, it hurt, too, but you knew where the bandages were, so it wasn't quite as frightening; you learned from your experiences and knew that you'd heal.

When you say, "If only something else had happened or been different, then ..." you think that things would have been better, but they might have been worse. Do what you can to improve your life, certainly, but don't waste time arguing with reality.

Your parents were in love with the unattainable. One of your dad's favorite songs, which he played beautifully (he taught himself to play the organ and the Hawaiian guitar) was "Beyond the Reef" (where the sea is dark and cold, my love has gone, and our dreams grow old … someday I know she'll come back again to me. Till then my heart will be beyond the reef). Was he thinking about your mom: beyond his reach, a failed marriage, a dream grown old?

And your mom's favorite song was "Somewhere My Love," there will be songs to sing; not here, not now, but somewhere. Was she thinking of Janine?

Here's my song for you, my dear inner child (and for the adult you became) for your unwavering determination to understand yourself and your place in the world, and your appreciation of life, "You are so Beautiful." I sing it, not to an impossible love, I sing it to myself (you're everything I've hoped for, you're everything I need, you are so beautiful to me).

39. Connecting the Dots

Speak, memory. — Vladimir Nabokov

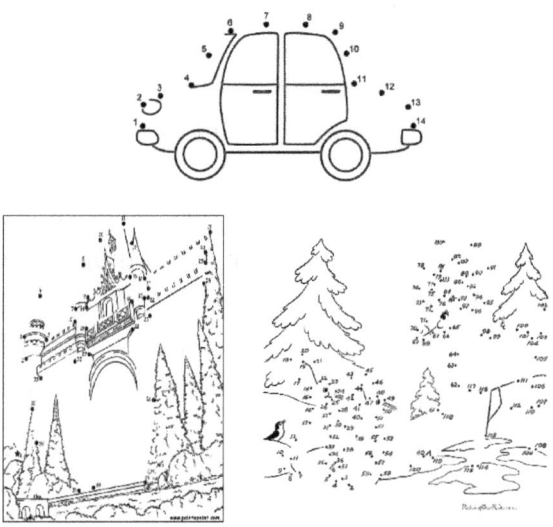

Connect-the-dots puzzles, easy, medium-hard, and difficult
https://www.thebalance.com/connect-dots-worksheets-1357606

The only connect-the-dot puzzles that I knew about and enjoyed as a child used a number sequence: 1, 2, 3, 4. Now I know that there were also puzzles in which the dots were arranged by twos: 2, 4, 6, 8; or by 10s: 10, 20, 30, 40; and sometimes alphabetically: a, b, c, d.

Connect the dots and a picture emerges. Trying to connect the dots for emotional events over a lifetime, to get a clear picture, can be more challenging. For that, you need the reliability of memory. My memory today of early events is sometimes sketchy; fortunately, I kept diaries and journals, had witnesses and, sometimes, my body remembered for me.

I could connect the dots regarding my social and performance anxiety to Dad's dire warnings about how untrustworthy people were, his horror stories, and "examples," like him holding me underwater at the lake after he promised he wouldn't go under, and firecrackers he set off behind me in the living room. I could also connect events to my anxiety, such as two car accidents later in life, each caused by other drivers. All those incidents put a bold exclamation point (**!**) on my anxiety.

My perfectionism came from a fear of death (Dad told me repeatedly that if I weren't really careful and did something stupid—or others did something stupid—I'd get seriously hurt or killed). Mom added to my anxiety by worrying frequently, "What will people think?"

More of a puzzle to me, as I tried to connect the dots, was my hypersexuality for about 10 years, starting when I was attending Eastern Michigan University and living in Ann Arbor, and continuing when I lived in San Francisco. To begin to connect those dots, I had to first consider the reliability of memory throughout my life, memories in general that had nothing to do with sex.

> When I was a teenager, I reached to get something out of the cupboard above the stove, and my robe brushed across the hot burner.
>
> I stood there in shock, my mind blank, and watched the fire climb up the side of my robe. Mom grabbed a dish towel and beat out the flames. Years later I reminded her of this, and she said, "Bill put out the flames."
>
> I distinctly remember seeing *her* rush at me with the towel. I emailed Bill and asked him who put out the flames; he never answered. He probably didn't remember the incident at all.

When I was 15 years old, I came upon the aftermath of a murder/suicide at a shopping mall near my house. A man was hosing blood and what looked like chunks of brains off the sidewalk. He told me that a man shot his ex-wife and then himself—in front of the couple's 15-year old daughter who'd been taken away.

As an adult, I don't remember seeing a body, but in my diary that day I wrote, "I saw a body lying in a pool of blood." I also wrote that I was with Lissa, my mom, and my brothers. The police screened off the area and wrapped the body in a blanket and carried it away on a stretcher.

Then connecting the dots becomes more challenging. Throughout the years Mom reiterated, "You could be so pretty if you'd just do something with your hair and wear a little makeup." She continued, "You have a long face. If you wear your hair shorter and with more body, it'll frame your face nicely," and "Do your boyfriends like your bangs that way?" She was trying to manipulate me into changing my hairstyle by suggesting that others would judge me if I didn't wear my hair the way *she* wanted me to.

So, not pretty enough for Mom; but wait, maybe too pretty, too feminine? She was a "tomboy" who was fearless, not afraid of heights or bears in the woods, and who threw a ball the "right" way (the way a boy does), whereas I was uncoordinated and afraid of a lot of things. Was I too much of a sissy for her, too "girly"? She told me once, during one of my visits after I taught my workshop, that she liked women who were "a little masculine." I wonder that if I were more like Mom's friends if she and I could have related better.

Then there was Dad, I was plenty pretty enough for him. Even though he yelled at me and called me names when I was growing up (followed by meals in our favorite restaurants, like an apology), I sometimes wondered if I was his favorite.

Had he infringed on my personal boundaries and depended on me too much by confiding in me some of the things that disturbed him the most at work? Did he realize how inappropriate it was to tell me dirty jokes and to tell my boyfriend that I turned him on?

Then, there was the day that we passed in the hallway and he put his finger down the front of my swimming suit. I pulled away and he shouted that as long as I lived in this house (our house) I would do as he said. He didn't touch me again, but I grew even more leery of him. Was I standing alone in the gap that Mom had left?

I became overly defensive and learned to distance myself. I struggled to remain "present" in my life and in my relationships.

I dissociated and spaced out when I felt stressed

My first kiss in high school made me feel real and alive, and I wanted more of that.

Then in college, having sex helped me to feel truly present and helped me to emerge from the cloud of anxiety, uncertainty, and apathy that engulfed me.

But was it more than that?

Dad's offhand sexual jokes and comments had an atmosphere of their own, like the odd, greenish-yellow color of the sky indicates that there's a tornado somewhere, not here exactly, but nearby. How often had he thought of me in *that* way or was he just expressing a passing thought? I buried his insinuations deep in the community of my unconscious thoughts, but they were there nevertheless, subtly affecting my peace of mind.

Choosing my sexual partners was a way to assert my independence, to turn my back on Dad, and to feel in control of who could have me and who couldn't.

I wondered if Dad had done something more terrible that I'd repressed. I didn't think so. He told me that he thought that I was a virgin until my first boyfriend in college.

And I remember all those years ago in the bathroom: blood after having had sex for the first time with my boyfriend. Blood; yes, *that* had been my first time. The extent of my relief signified the depth of my concern. Dad hadn't.

This time my *body* was the journal, my body kept the score.

All the dots connected

40. Eating God

We are stardust come to life. — Harold Bloom

I would rather live my life as if there is a God and find out there isn't, than live my life as if there isn't and die to find out there is. — Albert Camus

In the restaurant, I enjoy blackened catfish with Cajun seasonings for lunch and I think, *everything* is made of the genetic material of the Universe; there's a unifying truth behind and within all things, an implicate order that *is* all things. Atheists call it "science," physicists call it the "unified field," Hindus "Brahman," Buddhists the "Tao," Christians "God." Author Ernest Holmes stated that "We are all drops in one ocean," the waters of Life, and contain within us all the elements and characteristics of the greater ocean. My life works best when I believe that I'm part of it all.

Maybe when we die, we're not lost or destroyed, we're simply folded back into the cosmic mix, the deeper order from which we all came, or we go to "Heaven," as some believe. And if everything is really, truly "God," as I hope, then I'm eating God. I glance around the restaurant; everyone looks blasé, apathetic, and clueless. I want to shout, "Don't you know that you're eating God?" That'd shock the indifference out of them and inspire reverence for their food and for their lives—or maybe get me arrested for disturbing the peace.

I want to cry out, "Be more grateful, be more thrilled!" But if someone else shouted something like that in public, I'd think they were crazy, so I'll just be content to know it myself; and I am content, beyond content.

This "knowing" is exquisite. It reminds me of the time that Something summoned me to the mirror when I was a child and I sensed an inner spiritual "essence" when I peered into my eyes, and the time in church when a tenor sang a stirring solo and I felt suspended somewhere else in a radiant realm.

The feeling has no name, no rules or routine, no dogma, no religious denomination or affiliation, it just *is*, and I decide, right here and now, that my "religion" will be Life itself lived creatively with love, appreciation, and gratitude. And I will know that, feel that, every day.

I'm flooded with chills and awe; so thankful for the fish that's my lunch, and filled with love for my life, that I don't know how to respond when the server asks me if everything is all right.

41. Rockslide

It begins with a fault.
A slope.
And gravity.
With my eyes closed it sounds like a raging fire tearing a forest open, or a rushing waterfall crashing down a cliff. But it's neither fire nor water. It's a rockslide sucking me downhill fast—all the broken parts of me sliding together as one piece; the rocks loosen other rocks on the way down, my whole life joins the slip.

~~~

The room spins wildly out of control like in a blender, a free fall. I try to sit up in bed and slide onto the floor. My eyes won't focus or work together, they feel like "crazy eyes." Which end is up, I'm rocking, rising, falling, seasick, where is above/below, no left or right or in between. Still on the floor my hands grasp at the air, gigantic panels of color stagger across the room and behind the panels the walls whirl faster and *faster*, am I dying?

Mom, are you're kneeling beside me. When you fell a couple years ago and were on the floor for about 18 hours, I asked you what you thought as you lay there. You looked confused by the question—your tired, but still beautiful hazel eyes moving from side to side as if looking for an answer—or maybe you didn't want to talk about it. How did you feel two years later as your life slipped away for real, when your back stiffened, your shoulders hurt, you couldn't keep your breakfast down, and your heart lurched and turned on you, said no more! And you died in the car as Bill rushed you to the hospital.

Dad, you slumped at the kitchen table, 39 years earlier, a heart attack claimed you, too, tight as a fist in your chest; was there room in that clench to think of loved ones as you turned toward what, something—maybe an afterlife—or nothing?

Peter, I'm so sorry that you'll come home from your meeting and find me dead on the bedroom floor. My fingers splay out on the carpet, the last thing I'll see in my lifetime. When was the last time I vacuumed?

The dry-heaves surprise and offend me; I didn't expect dying to be this undignified. It's insulting. I expected to have a say, but my body has a mind of its own—whose mind is it?

My books, all my pretty ones—the seven published, did I communicate clearly what I wanted to say, and the six written, not published yet—I grieve the incompletions.

Friends, family, I didn't say good-bye; you don't know that I'm leaving forever. What are you doing as I die? Will you miss me? You will go on without me. And billions of people on the planet never knew that I existed—how small my footprint.

I feel so alone here on the floor. Has my life come down to this, to this room, these walls, and a high, beamed ceiling? I'm ready to turn myself over "from time to eternity."

Something in me pulls apart, separates, I rise upward swiftly, see the small, transparent kernel of my life, speeding away from me growing smaller, I see words floating randomly in the capsule shrinking fast. I see my life from a great distance, and I wonder, did it mean anything?

Something or Someone within me opts for life. Peter's not home to take me to the emergency room, and an ambulance might take too long, so I crawl to the phone and call my next-door neighbor Allene who rushes me to the hospital. She prays for me on the way—it's the one thing she knows for sure to do, I love her for that, for her generosity of spirit—one hand on the steering wheel, the other on my arm, praying for Divine intervention, stating emphatically, "This is *not* a heart attack, this is *not* a heart attack." She lets me out by the Emergency Room door. Someone slips a wheelchair under me and whisks me into an examining room where they put sticky EEG leads on me, swab my arm with alcohol, and start an IV.

Blood pressure: always freakishly low (once 80/35) skyrockets to 219/107. They pump anti-nausea, anti-dizziness solutions into the blue path of my vein, rehydrate me, check the monitors, do a drug test to look for overdose, and can't find anything wrong. But there is. Something. Very wrong.

I don't have a last will and testament, so Allene takes dictation. I moan, "I, being of sound mind ..." and laugh a little, I don't feel of sound mind; this all seems so ludicrous. I rattle off bank accounts, beneficiaries, and possessions. Taking her cue from my laughing, Allene says, "I'm writing in my own name as beneficiary."

She reaches Peter on his way home from his meeting and he comes to be with me in the ER. Several hours later the doctors release me—weak, shaken, and scared—no diagnosis, just a mandate to see my general physician.

I'm so puzzled. The ER doctors stabilized me enough to go home, but what happened?

I wait for my balance to return; it doesn't. I stop driving and move cautiously, never far from a wall, couch, or a counter to grab if I fall. I see my general physician a few days later and she speculates, "It might have been a virus that appears to be resolving itself." She doesn't hazard a guess as to what virus exactly. I do an Internet search, "How many viruses can infect people?" and get 71 results. Which one is "mine"?

I also research "extreme dizziness" and learn a new word for "crazy eyes," the involuntary, jerky eye motions that I experienced: nystagmus.

I post my symptoms on Facebook and a friend says that it might be an inner-ear problem: crystals, also known as "ear rocks," responsible for balance, sometimes move out of their chamber and go on a walkabout. But what can cause such a "rockslide"? Age, a blow to the head, leaning back for a prolonged time in a dentist's chair, or tipping your head back over the basin for a shampoo at a hair salon, which I did the afternoon before.

I see an ENT specialist, an "otolaryngologist," who confirms the ear-rock speculation, "Benign Paroxysmal Positional Vertigo."

He sees this condition frequently and doesn't seem worried. He has me lie face up on an examining table, performs the Epley maneuver—turns my head, rocks me back and forth and then quickly backwards and down with my head lower than my feet—and helps me slowly to a sitting position (I've since learned that the Half-somersault maneuver works just as well and is easier to do myself). My balance is restored. He advises, "This'll probably never happen again. Forget about it. Just go live your life."

But as with all rockslides, a new landscape has been created.

~~~

I feel my life winding down; I'm aware of this every day now. There are more years behind me than ahead.

I don't think about reincarnation. I've lived three lifetimes in this lifetime, which gives me plenty to think about: Michigan, when I was one person, San Francisco, when I was another, and Texas where, hopefully, I'm maturing.

One advantage to having lived a long life is having the opportunity to put things in perspective: the good, the bad, and the ugly, the wins and losses, the laughter and tears. I suspect that many people who die young don't have a chance to figure it all out. I don't have all the answers, just a few more than I did when I was younger.

As writer Zora Neale Hurston noted, "There are years that ask questions and years that answer." I made it to the answering years.

~~~

I don't think either of my parents had the dubious "gift" of a near-death experience or, as mine seemed, an out-of-life experience (another unattached cluster?). Dad died at breakfast and was dead on arrival at the hospital, and Mom died suddenly one morning, too.

I accept that I'm going to die, to let go of life, and it can come without any warning for any reason. There's a surrender that comes with that knowing and a kind of grace. My parents, here for a while and then gone. The wild birds I adore, here for a season and gone. I own nothing. I rent this life. I'm temporary. Any talent I have speaks through me.

So, did my life mean something? I'm pretty sure that the "Something" that lives me definitely has Meaning with a capital "M," but it's unfathomable with my limited consciousness and so, I glean a succession of meanings from it, each with a lowercase "m." From now on I'll live creatively and intelligently, minute by minute, with purpose and appreciation guided by life-affirming principles, such as compassion, creativity, enthusiasm, forgiveness, honesty, non-judgment, kindness, love, patience, respect, tact, tolerance, and trust. And I'll seek and revere these qualities in others. I'll be mindful that I am part of a common, yet magnificent, pattern called "Life."

As for "life after death," I pour over countless theories posed by philosophy, religion, physics, and science. I want to know the "how" of it. I love the idea of multiverses, parallel universes, and the "expanded present" that contains all of time—past, present, and future—in the moment.

When I drive by the senior-retirement community where I wanted to move Mom, just down the road from where I live, I get an eerie feeling that she moved there after all, but in a parallel universe. She's there, getting ready to go to the dining room for dinner with friends. But oh, how I miss her in human form.

I think that something continues after death, but I'd be amazed if it's the personality, which I suspect is an illusion.

Neuroscience localizes various components of near-death experiences (what people report seeing, hearing, and feeling) to the different parts of the brain affected at the time. Going down a "long dark tunnel" might be the result of decreased blood flow to the retinas or to the brain. Having an out-of-body experience or sensing a "presence" could mean that the temporoparietal region of the brain is being affected—or it could mean something else.

We have eyes and ears because there's *something* to see and hear *out there* in the world (or inside us) so maybe we also have a "God" part of the brain signifying that there's something spiritual and ongoing to feel and experience.

I've come to my own conclusions about an afterlife, not based on anything I've been told or read but based on what I feel. It might be "Heaven," a state of mind, or as the Persian prophet Baha'u'llah stated, "… a more abundant life."

If our loved ones are in heaven, then they're at peace because of the nature of heaven itself: a place or a state of mind in which one experiences a deep, everlasting sense of peace, free of emotional turmoil; they aren't angry at us back here on earth. If there's nothing beyond the grave, then they don't care; they're beyond caring.

In any case, I think that "heaven," the "afterlife," is going to be something unimagined so far by art, science, philosophy, or religion and I sense that it'll be okay.

~~~

With a new-found sense of peace, I glance out the window and see Rabbit enjoying breakfast at the edge of my neighbor's neatly

The Mortician's Child

mowed meadow. I turn away a couple seconds, turn back, and in Rabbit's place, a large hawk—also enjoying breakfast. But the hawk's meal is mouse size; a couple yards away, Rabbit sits motionless hiding in our meadow with its tall, merciful grass.

At night, Mediterranean Geckos shop for moths on my windowpane and during the day a larger lizard scurries up the tree while a Roadrunner—a bird known to kill and eat rattlesnakes—sips from the birdbath. Are the lizard and Roadrunner about to meet? If so, it'll be the end of the lizard. And freezing weather will claim the Roadrunner.

I sit with the knowledge that I, too, am alternately hunter and hunted; I pray for balance, for what's fair, and try to welcome impermanence or at least not fear it, and to be thankful that I got a chance to be part of it all. While I feel relatively safe from animals—coyotes, bobcats, and most people—I know that I'll become prey eventually to the process of life and death and there will be no hiding in meadows.

~~~

I go for a walk and admire the lilacs: kin to a world of purple, breakfast plums, and the faded carpet of a summer cottage, the bruise where he kissed hard; I crush a blossom between my fingers to see if it's the same all the way through—purple—and I remember the science of color: objects absorb every color there is and cast off the color we see. Lilacs are *all* colors *except* purple, a surface reflection, a discard. Is Life like that, too, a reflection of a deeper, all-inclusive implicit order, an absence we perceive?

~~~

Evening. I look up to see the trees huge and black against the deepest end of twilight, and there, the brilliant curve of a slender new moon, a bright harbor toward which I sail. And I remember last year being blind in one eye for a week after a failed laser procedure following cataract surgery; things were loose in there, in the cupboard of my eye, until the surgeon, a retina specialist—in an act so ordinary for him and singular for me—opened the door and swept the shelf clean of debris.

This morning, amazed at the gift of sight (distance vision now 20/20), and the gift of life, I watch a cardinal, "I'll fly to this tree, now I'll fly to that tree, and I'll fly to the next, and build my nest." Then blue jay, finch, and chickadee; all made of seeds, water, color, sun, and time.

If everything were static with no connection to anything else, if nothing ever grew or changed, there could be no life. And so, we build our temporary, interconnected lives, and once they're lived, they cannot be unlived. They exist forever. A life once lived is the *only* thing that Death *cannot* take away.

42. Like Medicine

Let us be grateful to people who make us happy, they are the charming gardeners who make our souls blossom. — Marcel Proust

The best time to make friends is before you need them.
— Ethel Barrymore

Write a book, get it published, have a book. Teach a class, get paid. Gather ingredients, cook or bake them, have an entrée. But what's the product of socializing, what's the point? I didn't like social gatherings. They were too "peopley" and seemed superficial.

I sat on the sidelines. I figured that whoever came over to talk to me was "assigned" to me by the Universe, an approach that paid off; I'd get a speaking engagement, have a good conversation, or sell a book (or 200, as was the case once when someone placed a big order). It was meant to be, I assured myself. It didn't occur to me at the time that just about *anyone* who came over would be interesting.

I was standoffish and introverted usually but experimented from time to time. Mystics say that there's no separation between anything, no duality, only one Mind from which all specifics spring, or as Freeman Dyson, the Nobel Prize winning physicist once said, "… there's only one of us." I explored that idea by imagining that what others were saying to me was me talking to myself. When I did that, it was spooky how connected I felt to them, almost obscenely so, erasing all mental boundaries and emotional privacy. Sometimes I commented on things that they said to me and they'd adamantly deny having said it, insisting that they only thought it. So, I retreated.

I puzzled my way through social interactions and netted a few friends. Peter hugs me, affectionately, "My autistic beauty." I correct him, "You mean artistic."

His look suggests otherwise, he meant autistic, to which I jokingly taunt, "I know you are, but what am I?"

My social awkwardness was conditioning, not neurological as autism is. It was Mom's perfectionism (what will people think?) and Dad's warnings (people will take advantage of you!). But how do I explain my sensitivity to light, sound, and people's thoughts (empathic?). And sometimes I identify with the feelings of others so strongly that I mistake them for my own; I also suspect that a person doesn't have to be present for me to experience what he or she is going through as though I'm experiencing it myself—like the time I felt like I was having a heart attack, only to find out that my Aunt Pat was dying of a heart attack at that same time. It's disconcerting.

I think back to when I was in college, feeling lonely, and walking through an arboretum. I saw a squirrel running around. I envied it and agonized, "Why was I created human?" There was an immediate reply, a gentle, confident voice to the right of me, a little lower than my shoulder. It answered, *for love.*

That experience stuck with me, so about 10 years ago I decided to "do a different," to risk participating more fully in life and become more sociable. I joined a mastermind group of women (Partners in Believing) from a Unity church I attended, and later, three monthly gatherings: a women's interfaith devotional (Fridays at Flora's), and two neighborhood get-togethers: "Women and Wine Wednesdays" and Book Club. I also meet friends for lunch, and Peter and I enjoy dinner with various couples.

And I joined Facebook—therapy, if I don't get too distracted and I cultivate friendships in the "real" world as well. Facebook lets me vent, laugh, connect, and share my hopes and concerns with others. It's validating, aggravating, funny, and thought provoking. I see more sides to people now, not just the bad as Dad emphasized. I can support people emotionally, receive support, and "block" people (which I did once) or "unfriend" them (twice), if need be. I have a lot of LGBTQ friends on Facebook and I know many personally. I love that they're "out" like Mom felt that she couldn't be.

While good mental health isn't as quantifiable as having books published, earning money, or making an entrée, it's a product, too.

~~~

I take a break from my writing and stop by a neighbor's house. She's sitting alone in her living room looking troubled. We visit a while. We don't talk about what's bothering us. For me it's the stress of trying to do too much at once, self-imposed deadlines, and feeling overwhelmed. For her, I suspect, it's her impending divorce.

As we visit, her face brightens, "I'm so glad that you came by. You're like medicine!"

I'm feeling better, too. Yes, we're like medicine for each other, remedies, "pharmacies" of wisdom, cheer, love, and compassion. Our experiences would lack depth and significance without friends being silly, being serious, being with us through the splendors and challenges of living, being there for us, and we for them.

We're *all* healers and can *all* be healed. Friendship is the medicine that makes the lonely, the uncertain, the wounded, whole.

Debbie, Kathleen, and Jean

43. The Final Conversation

Keep not your roses for my dead, cold brow, the way
is lonely, let me feel them now. — Arabella Smith

I don't want this to be a "gotcha" book. I hope I've healed enough to be objective and fair to everyone.

I realize now that Dad's angry, dire warnings and scare tactics were often intended to protect me, but his convoluted, complicated reasoning was impossible for me, a child, to understand.

He grew up in an unloving home, had a grim job, inhaled neurotoxins on a regular basis, was unhealthy, worked grueling hours, and came home to a wife who was in love with their daughter's sixth-grade teacher. And Mom was attracted to women in the 1940s and 50s, when being gay was considered a mental illness by psychiatrists, a crime by the state, and a sin by the church, and she married a man with intermittent rage. As their marriage spun out of control, they were weighted with the responsibility of raising three children. And I was a sensitive little girl overwhelmed by it all.

As I near the end of writing this book, I think I have a better understanding of Mom and Dad—and myself. I shake out the folds and pleats in our story and begin to see the natural lift and flow of the cloth and, by doing so, think more clearly. I felt guilty throughout my life that I didn't know how to comfort or console them, but it wasn't my job to manage their emotions; they chose how to think and feel and respond to their circumstances; just as I, who once felt the victim of my circumstances, can now choose to respond differently as an adult with greater understanding, insights, and compassion.

I weighed my guilt against what I felt were their limitations in parenting brought on by their own unsolved issues from their childhoods and their unmet needs. Things feel more "even" now, more equal and balanced. The weight begins to lift. I feel lighter. I don't think Mom and Dad would judge me now and I won't judge them, either. All accounts paid in full.

I glance at the obituaries and think about the grieving families. As a mortician's child, now an adult, I have an idea of the magnitude of each life lived, and I realize that we don't lose people we love forever—or lose ourselves—because *that part of us that lived cannot die*; it's safe forever.

I notice the tip of the scales in my own life as more people I know transition from "this side" to "the other side": grandparents, aunts and uncles, parents, a niece and nephew, increasing numbers of friends. They made it look easy, their departure from the physical. I sense them waiting for me; no rush.

If my dying should someday be agonizing or painful, I hope that a compassionate doctor or nurse will ease me gently along my way and let me "die with dignity." I have a "Do not resuscitate order." I'm an organ donor, although I don't want my lungs or liver to go to a smoker or an alcoholic. I want the rest of me to be cremated.

My brother Bill plans to visit Dad's grave marker in Maine. Matt already went and put photos of his daughters on the flat stone in the grass, "There were tears," he said.

I'm not going. I pilgrimage back in time whenever I work on this book. It's a way to remember, honor, understand, and forgive.

As I drift off to sleep, Dad and I speak in my mind as though he's still alive.

Kathleen L. Hawkins

He asks, "Do you know what people want more than anything in the world?"

"No, what?"

"Resurrection; second chances. They're desperate for second chances and don't even know it until someone dies."

I remember him saying of himself, "One day I'll go just like that," and he snapped his fingers. And he did. He went just like that.

If I'd known then that he was going to die so suddenly that morning—without any warning, a good-bye, or a word of parental advice—would I have done anything differently? Would the insignificant have become preciously significant? Would we have tried harder? How frequently, in careless, thoughtless little ways, we abandoned each other.

And I didn't know that he'd be resurrected, but it'd go awry. He didn't ascend into heaven or descend into hell; he rose again in his own daughter's heart because I left an empty, unfinished place there. He rose in me and filled me with his anger, sadness, anxiety, and pain. It's a grief reaction, how the personality of the deceased can rise in a survivor. It's a way for the living to keep the dead alive, and a way to be possessed.

His resurrection in me was so fierce that I fought a low-grade depression and free-floating anxiety for years, and eventually half believed he was still alive, but living in another city. I imagined that I'd see him on one of my business trips, but I'd be riding on a train or a bus or in a taxi and wouldn't be able to reach him.

My "exorcism" took years until my grief unwound and played itself out through writing this book; I released him and, in doing so, released myself.

In my imagined conversation with him before I go to sleep, I whisper, "Why are people so desperate for second chances?"

His voice is far away, "To learn how to love."

And I understand now what he had trouble articulating when I was younger. I tell him, "Instead of yelling at me so much when I was growing up, why didn't you just tell me that you loved me? Why didn't you say that you were worried about losing me and you'd miss me when I moved to San Francisco?"

He's quiet for a long time, and then says, "I love you. I would have missed you when you moved to San Francisco."

"Oh, how I wish that you'd lived long enough for me to learn to love you, too. I was going to write a letter to you when I got to San Francisco and settled in. I was going to try to explain everything that I was feeling. I realize now that *this* book is *that* letter."

Our conversation works me like a drug, spreads evenly throughout my body, and puts me into a deep, peaceful sleep. And I dream that I'm riding on a train rolling through the countryside. At one station, I see Dad standing alone on a platform as I pass. He lifts his face to meet mine and I see that the pain is no longer in his eyes and, upon awakening, discover that it's no longer in mine.

Epilogue

There is my truth; now tell me yours.
— Friedrich Nietzsche

Links
All links are active at the time of this writing

Kathleen L. Hawkins
www.WinningSpirit.com

Restaurants
- Big Boy https://en.wikipedia.org/wiki/Big_Boy_Restaurants
- Howard Johnson's https://en.wikipedia.org/wiki/Howard_Johnson%27s
- Sindbad's on the Detroit River http://sindbads.com

Half-somersault maneuver to treat BPPV vertigo (the first 10 seconds of the video "spin" so don't watch it if you're sensitive)
https://www.youtube.com/watch?v=mQR6b7CAiqk

Lakes
- Cass Lake, MI https://www.youtube.com/watch?v=i97VZaQSYHU&list=PLEB945A0EAF1B5364
- Kensington Lake, MI https://www.youtube.com/watch?v=NsJ5a4snqsc
- Black Lake, MI https://www.vrbo.com/vacation-rentals/usa/michigan/northeast/black-lake
- Higgins Lake, MI https://www.youtube.com/watch?v=22AxapdMyYE
- Grapevine Lake, TX https://www.youtube.com/watch?v=uqg4MksBO00

Bob-Lo Island Amusement Park and Steamships
- http://bobloboat.com/history.html; http://www.boblosteamers.com
- https://www.youtube.com/watch?v=jhjzjlMGPDU

Universities
- Eastern Michigan https://www.youtube.com/watch?v=5wan83LgBRE
- San Francisco State https://www.youtube.com/watch?v=1L6kVqgyqx8
- Worsham College of Mortuary Science, Illinois http://www.worshamcollege.com

Eastern Michigan Asylum for the Insane (Clinton Valley Center), Pontiac, MI
- https://en.wikipedia.org/wiki/Clinton_Valley_Center
- www.rootsweb.ancestry.com/~asylums/pontiac_mi/index.html
- https://www.youtube.com/watch?v=esZeD_c2IO4

Kathleen L. Hawkins

Women's Army Auxiliary Corps (WAAC)
- https://en.wikipedia.org/wiki/Women%27s_Army_Corps
- http://chnm.gmu.edu/courses/rr/s01/cw/students/leeann/historyandcollections/history/lrnmrewwiiwac.html
- http://en.wikipedia.org/wiki/Women's_Army_Corpsslowly

Music
- Dad's favorite: "Beyond the Reef" https://www.youtube.com/watch?v=LZPWAYEshTo; lyrics https://www.youtube.com/watch?v=i1VnRvq90Wk
- Mom's favorites, "Somewhere my Love" https://www.youtube.com/watch?v=3RGWE6zJKXk; lyrics https://www.youtube.com/watch?v=65ACK8LptHY; hymns: "In the Garden" https://www.youtube.com/watch?v=pAlNwE6q8z0 and "Just a Closer Walk with Thee" https://www.youtube.com/watch?v=hrM1aWtYpys
- My favorites, "You are so Beautiful": https://www.youtube.com/watch?v=bor44-RK44U; "Bridge Over Troubled Water" https://www.youtube.com/watch?v=Ho92k2CKNh0; "I Saw You Comin' Back to Me" https://www.youtube.com/watch?v=0NdvMT32skw; One Flew Over the Cuckoo's Nest (movie opening theme with a musical saw) https://www.youtube.com/watch?v=uWsz5xMJF6k

LGBTQ History and References
- Glossary http://lgbtqia.ucdavis.edu/educated/glossary.html
- Timeline/LGBTQ history https://en.wikipedia.org/wiki/Timeline_of_LGBT_history
- Supervisor Dianne Feinstein announces the assassination of Milk and Moscone https://www.youtube.com/watch?v=5NikqzmwbgU
- Stonewall Riots (1969) explained https://www.youtube.com/watch?v=7ZrQeNBMqOk
- Documentary: How We got Gay https://www.youtube.com/watch?v=foQrmKRUFgg
- Movie: Prayers for Bobby https://www.youtube.com/watch?v=pvdxDsRX7hg
- Books: *Families like Mine*, *Milk,* and *The Other Side of the Closet*

Spiritual Influences
- Joy Farm (Ministry of the High Watch), Kent, CT, an artists' and writers' retreat and metaphysical center where Mom and her sister, Charlene, lived with Grandfather; History of High Watch http://highwatchrecovery.com/history/; the farm was later donated to Alcoholics Anonymous http://highwatchrecovery.com; High Watch gallery http://highwatchrecovery.com/gallery/
- Salvation Army Harbor Light, San Francisco where I worked for four years https://www.youtube.com/watch?v=_pDr7hutzCA
- New Thought Resources http://servingnewthought.org; Centers for Spiritual Living http://csl.org; Unity http://www.unity.org; Science of Mind 10 Core Concepts (PDF) http://scienceofmind.com/wp-content/uploads/2016/06/10_core_concepts.pdf

Thoughts, Blogs, and Resources about Death
- Caleb Wilde, *Confessions of a Funeral Director* https://www.calebwilde.com
- Pamela Skjolsvik, "The Death Writer," author of *Death Becomes Us* and *Forever 51* https://www.pamelaskjolsvik.com/books
- The Death Positive Movement http://www.orderofthegooddeath.com/resources/death-positive-movement; The Order of the Good Death: funeral industry professionals, academics, and artists who explore ways to prepare a death-phobic culture for inevitable mortality http://www.orderofthegooddeath.com/death-positive

www.ingramcontent.com/pod-product-compliance
Lightning Source LLC
Chambersburg PA
CBHW061430040426
42450CB00007B/985